Conjoint Family Therapy

Conjoint Family Therapy

Third Edition

by Virginia Satir

SCIENCE AND BEHAVIOR BOOKS, INC.

Palo Alto, California

Library of Congress Number 82-061781

ISBN 8314-0063-3

Editing and design by Rain Blockley
Cover design by Lois Stanfield
(Original cover design by Nord Graphic Art Studio)
Typesetting by ComCom
Printed in the United States of America

CONTENTS

PREFACE

Welcome to the third edition of *Conjoint Family Therapy*. This edition is both a revision and a vehicle for new material. Parts One through Three (the original book) are largely unchanged except for chapter XII, "Using a Family Life Chronology"—which has been expanded and modified slightly—and chapter XV, "Integrating Models and Disciplines," which has been updated.

Part Four presents two new chapters. The first, "When I Meet a Person," is a subjective account of my initial interview with a family. The chapter answers many of the questions I am often asked, and I think therapists will find it of great interest. It also is a bridge to my later book, *Peoplemaking*. The communication stances and patterns that I describe in *Peoplemaking* play an important role in my initial perceptions of this family. Recognizing these communication postures helps me to design appropriate exercises or interventions. Once the family members are aware of their own stances, they have opened the door to change.

The second new chapter describes a new dimension in my family therapy experience. Just as this book originally grew out of the then revolutionary idea that individuals could be treated in the presence of their families, "Involving the Larger System" recounts a project in which sixty families were treated within the context of their *community*. Since the project's sponsor, the state of Virginia, is still conducting follow-up studies, my account is not a final analysis. Instead, it captures my excitement about the approach and about the work I did with the nine other members of my team. The project's results will have many implications for family therapists, and readers may want to consider using this "larger systems" approach if they have the opportunity.

An "Author's Note" and a new bibliography complete this new edition. The note describes my other training materials and how they can be used in conjunction with this book. It also provides information on Avanta, a training program I created.

*   *   *   *   *

This book grew out of demands for teaching materials for a course in Family Dynamics which I taught to psychiatric residents at the Illinois State Psychiatric Institute in Chicago from 1955 to 1958. Since that time, many of my colleagues from the fields of medicine, psychiatry, psychology, social work, nursing, education, anthropology and sociology have expressed interest in my training programs in family therapy and have encouraged me to expand my initial training outlines and put them in book form. This book is the result, and represents the conclusions I have reached to date on the difficult and challenging subject of conjoint family therapy.

Many major contributions have been made to the use of the family as a therapeutic unit by people who saw behavior as a result of interactional experience in addition to intra-psychic forces. I was one of many who experimented with observing the person labeled "schizophrenic" *in the presence of his family,* rather than by individual treatment alone.

The germ of my particular theory and practice grew out of a new appraisal of the meaning of relatives' calls to me about the "patient" I was seeing. These calls were ostensibly in the form of complaints about the patient, or about my handling, or reports about things they thought I should know about. In traditional psychotherapeutic practice, I had been taught to view any attempt by a relative to communicate with the therapist as a potentially dangerous obstacle to the treatment relationship. As I began to try to understand the meaning of these calls, I saw that there were at least two messages conveyed in them: one about the pain or trouble that the relative observed in the patient, and one about the pain and trouble in himself.

The next step was to see that the call contained not only an offer of help to the patient, but also a request for help for the relative disguised as a threat. It was then impossible not to recognize that there was an essential relationship between a patient and his family. While I had known this at some level, it was now explicit. Furthermore, it became clear that any individual's behavior is a response to the complex set of regular and predictable "rules" governing his family group, though these rules may not be consciously known to him or the family. From this point of view, we can begin to stop seeing relatives' activities only as dangers, and look at them as forces for growth and indications of the power of interactional transactions in relation to shaping the behavior of the individuals that are a part of that family system.

Most family therapists today agree more or less on how the family systems operate. However, there are now wide differences in ways of modifying these systems. In fact, today—thirty years after family therapy began—we hear talk of "schools" of family therapy. This is reminiscent of the days when a student of human behavior had to choose whether he or she would follow Freud, Jung, or Adler. At that time (forty years ago), it was considered unprofessional to use any ideas that were not part of one's "leader's" methods or approach. It was bad to be eclectic. We are not quite so rigid today. The last word on family therapy has yet to be spoken. It behooves all of us to continue being students. My recommendation is that we free ourselves to look anywhere and to use what seems to fit. This makes each of us a continually growing entity.

In this vein, I want to emphasize that I offer this book as a conceptual frame around which to organize your data and your impressions, rather than something to be memorized and followed as though it were a recipe. It is a suggested path. The best approach to any situation will be determined by its particular circumstances. It is very important that therapists be flexible and free to adopt whatever is necessary and appropriate under those circumstances.

This book is primarily intended to prepare students for effective family therapy work and to refresh "old pros" about parts that are easy to forget. For this reason, I kept the informal outline format of the training manual from which this book originated. At this point, family therapy has been further explored. We are much farther along in both our knowledge about how family systems operate, and I hope that the book may also serve as a catalyst for innovations in both clinical practice and research.

Virginia S. Satir

ACKNOWLEDGMENTS

No man develops by himself. The evolution of this book and the ideas contained herein present a concrete example of this fact. Therefore, to all persons with whom I have had the experience of an interaction throughout my lifetime, I extend thanks for the enrichment they have given me.

Opportunities for clarification of my thinking have been many and rich through the questions of people who have elected to be in my training seminars or who have invited me as a consultant all over the United States and four other continents. To the persons who have sought my treatment services during the past forty-one years, I wish to extend special thanks. Without them, I would have had no way of knowing whether my ideas had any particular relevance.

For the encouragement I received while teaching at the Illinois State Psychiatric Institute, Chicago, Illinois, I should like to thank Dr. Kalman Gyarfas, then director of the Institute, and Miss Pauline Peters, director of social work at Chicago State Hospital, where the newly formed Institute was then housed.

My original ideas were greatly expanded and altered through my intimate professional association with Dr. Don Jackson, Gregory Bateson, Jay Haley, John Weakland, Dr. William Fry, Dr. Jules Riskin, Dr. Robert Spitzer, and others at the Mental Research Institute, Palo Alto, California.

To my many other colleagues who were also engaged in the exciting work of studying family interaction and its relationship to the development of health and illness, I wish to express my appreciation for their willingness to offer me the findings of their research. Among these many persons were: Dr. Murray Bowen, Dr. Warren Brodey, Dr. Victor Freeman, Dr. S. Minuchin, Dr. E. Auerswald, Dr. Otto Pollak, Dr. Eric Berne, and Dr. S. I. Hayakawa.

In addition, I should like to acknowledge the generous financial help given me for the first edition by the following foundations: the National Institute of Mental Health for their Small Grant and Training Grant; Mrs. H. L. McIntyre for her gift from the Robert C. Wheeler Foundation, and the Louis W. and Maud Hill Family Foundation for their grant to the Family Project.

The first edition would never have come into being without the able assistance of Barbara Francisco, who spent many hours over a two year period listening to tapes of my teaching and treatment sessions in order to pull the material together. To Lynn Hoffman, who lent her excellent editorial skills to putting the manuscript in its final form, and to Camille Ball, who volunteered her help in typing the manuscript, I give special thanks. I wish also to thank Dee Barlow Krueger for her contribution to the preparation and writing of the Revised Edition.

Since the original publication of this book, I have traveled widely and shared experiences with many people. My thanks go to all of them, and particularly to Ruth Topping, Fritz Perls, Michael Murphy, and Richard Price.

As my experience worldwide has continued to deepen, broaden, and lengthen, I have been privileged to be in contact with the emerging leaders in the field of holistic health, which is opening up vistas never before dreamed of. Brugh Joy, M.D.; Ken Pelletier, Ph.D.; Irving Ogle, M.D.; Norman Shealy, M.D.; Carl Simonton, M.D., and Stephanie Simonton; Elisabeth Kubler-Ross, M.D.; Al Huang; Stan Grof, M.D.; Bob Ornstein, Ph.D.; Lama Govinda; Alyce and Elmer Green, Ph.D.s; Jack Schwarz; Ida Rolf; Fredrik Lionel; Karl Pribram; and Marcel Vogel are outstanding among the people who have especially touched me in ways that informed and stimulated me toward new discoveries and possibilities.

I want to extend special thanks to Robert Spitzer, M.D., and his capable editor, Rain Blockley, for literally riding herd on me to carve out the time to do this revised edition.

Finally, I feel a deep gratitude for the support and stimulation of the members of Avanta and of the International Human Learning Resource Network (IHLRN), who have joined in the dream of how to help people become more fully human.

KEY TO ABBREVIATIONS

The following abbreviations have been used
throughout the text.

I.P.	—	Identified Patient
Th	—	Therapist
H	—	Husband
W	—	Wife
F	—	Father
M	—	Mother
S	—	Son
D	—	Daughter

References cited are included in the numbered
bibliography. In the text, these sources are
indicated by their respective bibliography numbers
(in parentheses) for easy reference.

PART ONE: FAMILY THEORY

CHAPTER I

Why Family Therapy?

1. Family therapists deal with family pain.

   a. When one person in a family (the patient) has pain which shows up in symptoms, all family members are feeling this pain in some way.

   b. Many therapists have found it useful to call the member who carries the symptom the "Identified Patient," or "I.P.," rather than to join the family in calling him "the sick one," or "the different one," or "the one who is to blame."

   c. This is because the therapist sees the Identified Patient's symptoms as serving a family function as well as an individual function.

2. Numerous studies have shown that the family behaves as if it were a unit. In 1954 Jackson introduced the term "family homeostasis" to refer to this behavior (39).

   a. According to the concept of family homeostasis, the family acts so as to achieve a balance in relationships.

  b. Members help to maintain this balance overtly and covertly.

  c. The family's repetitious, circular, predictable communication patterns reveal this balance.

  d. When the family homeostasis is precarious, members exert much effort to maintain it.

3. The marital relationship influences the character of family homeostasis.

  a. The marital relationship is the axis around which all other family relationships are formed. The mates are the "architects" of the family.

  b. A pained marital relationship tends to produce dysfunctional parenting.

4. The Identified Patient is the family member who is most obviously affected by the pained marital relationship and most subjected to dysfunctional parenting.

  a. His symptoms are an "SOS" about his parents' pain and the resulting family imbalance.

  b. His symptoms are a message that he is distorting his own growth as a result of trying to alleviate and absorb his parents' pain.

5. Many treatment approaches are called "family therapy" but differ from the definition which will be presented here, since they are oriented primarily to family members as individuals rather than to the family as a unit as well. For example:

  a. Each family member may have his own therapist.

  b. Or family members may share the same therapist, but the therapist sees each member separately.

   c.   Or the patient may have a therapist who occasionally sees other family members "for the sake of" the patient.

6. A growing body of clinical observation has pointed to the conclusion that family therapy must be oriented to the family as a whole. This conviction was initially supported by observations showing how family members respond to the individual treatment of a family member labeled as "schizophrenic." But further studies showed that families with a delinquent member respond in similar ways to the individual treatment of this member. In both cases it was found that:

   a.   Other family members interfered with, tried to become part of, or sabotaged the individual treatment of the "sick" member, as though the family had a stake in his sickness.

   b.   The hospitalized or incarcerated patient often got worse or regressed after a visit from family members, as though family interaction had a direct bearing on his symptoms.

   c.   Other family members got worse as the patient got better, as though sickness in one of the family members were essential to the family's way of operating.

7. These observations led many individually-oriented psychiatrists and researchers to re-evaluate and question certain assumptions (109, 110, 114, 140, 142, 146, 162).

   a.   They noted that when the patient was seen as the victim of his family, it was easy to overidentify with and overprotect him, overlooking the fact that:
      — Patients are equally adept at victimizing other family members in return.
      — Patients help to perpetuate their role as the sick, different, or blamed one.

   b.   They noted how heavily transference was relied on in order to produce change.
      — Yet perhaps much of the patient's so-called transference was really an appropriate reaction to the

therapist's behavior in the unreal, noninteractive, therapeutic situation.

— In addition, there was a greater chance that the therapeutic situation would perpetuate pathology, instead of presenting a new state of affairs which would introduce doubts about the old perceptions.

— If some of the patient's behavior did represent transference (that is, his characteristic way of relating to his mother and father), why shouldn't the therapist help the patient deal with the family more directly, by seeing both the patient and his family together?

c. They noted that the therapist tended to be more interested in the patient's fantasy life than in his real life. But even if they were interested in the patient's real life, as long as they saw just the patient in therapy, they had to rely on his version of that life or try and guess what was going on in it.

d. They noted that in trying to change one family member's way of operating they were, in effect, trying to change the whole family's way of operating.

— This put the burden of family change-agent on the patient all by himself rather than on all family members.

— The patient was already the family member who was trying to change the family's way of operating, so when he was urged to increase his efforts, he only received a more intense criticism from the family. This also led him to feel even more burdened and less able.

8. Aside from all these observations, once therapists started to see the whole family together, other aspects of family life which produced symptoms were revealed, aspects which had been largely overlooked. Other investigators of family interaction were making similar discoveries. As Warren Brodey sees it, the mates act differently with the normal sibling than they do with the symptomatic sibling (27):

. . . the parents in the presence of the "normal" sibling are able to relate with a freedom, flexibility, and breadth of awareness that one finds hard to believe, considering the limitations that exist in the relationship between the parents when involved with the symptomatic sibling. The pathological ways of relating seem to be focused within the relationship with the symptomatic member. One wonders how this has come about.

9. But those psychiatrists who became increasingly devoted to family therapy were not the first to recognize the interpersonal nature of mental illness. Sullivan and Fromm-Reichmann, along with many other psychiatrists, psychologists, and social workers, were pioneers in this area of discovery. The Child Guidance movement was another important development which helped break the tradition of singling out just one family member for treatment (41).

   a. Child Guidance therapists included both mother and child in treatment, even though they still tended to see mother and child in separate treatment sessions.

   b. They also increasingly recognized the importance of including the father in therapy, though they found him hard to reach, and generally failed to engage him in the therapy process.
      — Therapists reported that the father felt parenting was his wife's job more than his; if the child acted disturbed, his wife was the one who should be seen.
      — The Child Guidance therapists, being mother-child oriented anyway, tended to agree with the father's reasoning, so they could not easily convince him that his role in the family was important to the health of his child.
      — Child Guidance Clinics remained primarily focused on "mothering," even though they increasingly recognized the importance of "fathering." And whether or not they included the father in their thinking, they continued to focus on the husband and wife as parents of the child rather than as mates to each other. Yet it has been repeatedly noted how critically the marital relationship affects parenting. Murray Bowen writes, for example (25):

        The striking observation was that when the parents were emotionally close, more invested in each other than either was in the patient, the patient improved. When *either* parent became more emotionally invested in the patient than in the other parent, the patient immediately and automatically regressed. When the parents were emotionally close, they could do no wrong in their "management" of the patient. The patient responded well to firmness, permissiveness, punishment, "talking it out," or any other management approach. When the parents were "emotionally divorced," any and all "management approaches" were equally unsuccessful.

10. Family therapists have found it easier to interest the husband in family therapy than in individual therapy. This is because the family therapist is himself convinced that both architects of the family must be present.

   a. Once the therapist convinces the husband that he is essential to the therapy process, and that no one else can speak for him or take his place in therapy *or* in family life, he readily enters in.

   b. The wife (in her role as mother) may initiate family therapy, but once therapy is under way, the husband becomes as involved as she does.

   c. Family therapy seems to make sense to the whole family. Husband and wife say: "Now, at last, we are together and can get to the bottom of this."

11. Right from the first contact, family therapists operate from certain assumptions about why a family member has sought therapeutic help.

   a. Usually the first contact is made because someone outside the family has labeled Johnny as disturbed. This first contact will probably be made by an anxious wife (we will call her Mary Jones), acting in her role as mother of a disturbed child, Johnny. The child is disturbed, so she, the mother, must be to blame.

   b. But Johnny was probably exhibiting disturbed behavior long before he became labeled disturbed by someone outside the family.

c.   Until the outsider (often a teacher) labeled Johnny as disturbed, members of the Jones family probably acted as though they did not notice Johnny's behavior; his behavior was appropriate because it served a family function.

d.   Usually some event has occurred which has precipitated symptoms in Johnny, symptoms which make the fact that he is disturbed obvious to outsiders. These events are:
— Changes from outside the nuclear family: war, depression, etc.
— Changes in the two families of origin: sickness of a grandmother, financial distress of a grandfather, etc.
— Someone enters or leaves the nuclear family: grandmother comes to live with the family, the family takes on a boarder, the family adds to its membership with the birth of another child, a daughter gets married.
— Biological changes: a child reaches adolescence, mother reaches menopause, father is hospitalized.
— Major social changes: a child leaves home to attend school, the family moves to a new neighborhood, father gets a job promotion, son goes to college.

e.   These events can precipitate symptoms because they require the mates to integrate the changes. This requirement puts an extra strain on the marital relationship because it calls for a redefinition of family relationships and thus affects family balance.

f.   The family homeostasis can be functional (or "fitting") for members at some periods of family life and not at other periods, so events affect members differently at different times.

g.   But if one member is affected by an event, all are to some degree.

12. After the first contact with Mary Jones, the therapist may speculate about the relationship between Mary and her husband, whom we will call Joe. If it is correct to assume that a dysfunctional marital relationship is the main

contributor to symptoms in a child, the relationship between the mates will be the therapist's first concern.

a. What kind of people are Mary and Joe? What kind of families did they come from?
   — Once they were two separate people who came from different family environments.
   — Now they are the architects of a new family of their own.

b. Why, out of all the people in the world, did they choose each other as mates?
   — How they chose each other gives clues to why they may now be disappointed with each other.
   — How they express their disappointment with each other gives clues to why Johnny needs to have symptoms in order to hold the Jones family together.

CHAPTER II

Low Self-Esteem and Mate Selection

1. A person with low self-esteem has a great sense of anxiety and uncertainty about himself.

    a. His self-esteem is based to an extreme extent on what he thinks others think of him.

    b. His dependence on others for his self-esteem cripples his autonomy and individuality.

    c. He disguises his low self-esteem from others, especially when he wants to impress others.

    d. His low self-esteem comes from his growing-up experiences which never led him to feel that it is good to be a person of one sex in relation to a person of the other.

    e. He has never really separated from his parents, that is, arrived at a relationship of equality with them.

2. A person with low self-esteem has high hopes about what he can expect from others, but he also has great fears; he is only too ready to expect disappointment and to distrust people.

    a.   When Mary and Joe enter therapy, the therapist will try to find out what they hoped for and feared from each other in their early courtship period, because:
— It was not an accident that they selected one another as mates; there was something they saw in each other which seemed to fit their high hopes.
— There was also something they saw in each other (but did not permit themselves to openly acknowledge) which seemed to corroborate their fears or distrust. The therapist will find them inducing the feared, expected behavior in the other as if they were trying to get the uncertainty over with (as if they were trying to fulfill their own prophesies).
— Their marital relationship will, in many respects, duplicate or be diametrically opposed to the relationship which each saw existing between his own parents.

3. Perhaps Mary and Joe each saw what he hoped for in the other because each was behaving at the level of his defenses rather than at the level of his inner feelings.

    a.   Joe acted self-confident and strong on the outside but felt uncertain, helpless, and frightened on the inside. When Mary looked at Joe she could say: "Here is a strong person who can take care of me."

    b.   Mary acted self-confident, outgoing, talkative on the outside but felt uncertain, helpless, frightened on the inside. When Joe looked at Mary he could say: "Here is a strong person who can take care of me."

    c.   After marriage, each found the other was not the strong person for which he hoped. Frustration, disappointment, anger, were bound to result.

4. One might wonder how Mary and Joe managed to find a mate if they had such low self-esteem and so little trust.

    a.   Once puberty brought adult sexuality to the fore, they risked relationship in spite of all their fears.

    b.   Also, they were in love which, for the time, enhanced their self-esteem and made each feel complete. Each said: "You seem to value me . . . I am lucky to have you . . . I need you in order to survive . . . I am complete if you are around."

   c. Both ended up living for each other and, in doing so, entered into a "survival pact." Each said privately to himself: "If I run out of supplies I will take from you. You will have enough, in an emergency, to serve us both."

5. The trouble was, when choosing each other as mates, that Mary and Joe did not communicate their fears to each other.

   a. Joe feared that Mary would not love him if she knew about his worthlessness (and vice versa).
    — It was as if Joe said privately to himself: "I must not reveal that I am nothing. Nor must I reveal the fact that I secretly expect all women to be unfair, irrational, sarcastic, stubborn, domineering. I must not reveal my belief that the only way to survive with a woman is to withdraw from the scene and let her run the show."
    — It was as if Mary said privately to herself: "I must not reveal that I am nothing. Nor must I reveal that I secretly expect all men to be stingy, irresponsible, indecisive, weak, and let women carry the burden. I must not reveal my belief that the only way to survive with a man is to be ready to shoulder the burden the minute he complains."

   b. Yet in spite of what each privately expected from the other and thought of himself, each also felt he must be what he thought the other saw in him because he had put the other in charge of his self-esteem.
    — When Mary let Joe know that she saw him as strong, Joe at first saw Mary's perception as strengthening; he could feel strong because she saw him as strong (and vice versa).
    — This kind of relationship can be maintained until an environmental stress or a decision-making requirement challenges Mary and Joe's ability to cope. Only then does strength begin to look like a cover-up for weakness or like domination.

    c.   Neither Mary nor Joe can ask what the other expects, hopes for, fears, because both feel they are supposed to be able to guess about what is going on inside the other. (In other words, it is as if both live by a crystal ball.)

    d.   Since each operates from the assumption that he must please the other, neither of them can communicate when he is displeased with the other, or acknowledge disagreement or criticism directly. They operate as though they must be indistinguishable from each other. They live as though they were on the same bloodstream, on the same survival pipeline. For example, I once had a marital pair who sat at the therapy table throughout the first two sessions with their arms intertwined, while their child, experiencing the tragedy of it all, sat across from them hallucinating.

6. In effect, Mary and Joe married to "get."

    a.   Each wanted the other's esteem of him. (Both also wanted society's esteem of them: "One should get married. I have now succeeded.")

    b.   Each wanted the other's qualities which he felt he lacked (qualities which he tried to make a part of himself).

    c.   Each wanted an extension of himself.

    d.   Each wanted an omnipotent, omniscient, selfless, "good" parent in the other, and wanted to avoid the omniscient, omnipotent "bad" parent.

CHAPTER III

Different-ness and Disagreements

1. When Mary and Joe married they did not realize that they would have to "give" as well as get.

   a. Each felt he had nothing to give.

   b. Each felt he should not be expected to give because the other was an extension of the self.

   c. If either did give, he did so grudgingly or anxiously or self-sacrificingly because neither really expected to get.

2. When Mary and Joe discover, after marriage, that the other is "different" from what each expected during courtship, they become disillusioned. What they actually now see in the other are the twenty-four-hour-a-day characteristics which do not usually show up during courtship, and consequently do not fit their expectations.

   a. Mary puts her hair in curlers when she goes to bed at night.

   b. Mary persistently serves overcooked beans.

    c.   Joe leaves his dirty socks strewn around the room.

    d.   When Joe goes to bed at night he snores.

3. When Mary and Joe discover, after marriage, that they are different in ways which seem to take away rather than add to them, they see each other in a new light.

    a.   "Different-ness" looks bad because it leads to disagreement.

    b.   Disagreement reminds them both that the other is not an extension of the self but is separate.

4. I mean the term "different-ness" to cover the whole area of individuality, how each person is innately different from every other person.

    a.   People can be physically different (A is tall, B short; A is male, B female).

    b.   People can have different personalities or temperament (A is excitable and outgoing, B placid and reserved).

    c.   People can have different educational backgrounds and abilities (A knows about physics, B about music; A has good tool dexterity, B can sing).

    d.   The presence of different-ness in another can be used destructively, rather than as an opportunity for enrichment.

5. The particular kinds of different-ness which bother Mary and Joe the most are:

    a.   Different preferences, wishes, habits, tastes (A likes to go fishing, B hates it; A likes the window open at night, B likes it closed).

    b.   Different expectations and opinions (A expects women to be strong, B expects men to be strong; A has religious convictions, B doesn't).

6. Different-ness which leads to a conflict of interests (disagreement) is seen as an insult and as evidence of being unloved.

    a.   It seems to threaten autonomy and self-esteem.

    b.   One may have to give while the other gets. Yet there isn't enough to go around. Who will get what is available?

    c.   Before marriage, each thought the other had enough for two people. Now, when disagreement comes up, it looks as if there may not even be enough for one.

7. If Mary and Joe had self-esteem, each would be able to trust the other.

    a.   Each would feel confident in his ability to get from the other.

    b.   Each could even wait to get.

    c.   Each could give to the other without himself feeling robbed.

    d.   Each could use the different-ness of the other as an opportunity for growth.

8. Mary and Joe lack trust.

    a.   Each feels he has barely enough to sustain his own life, let alone the other's life.

    b.   Each behaves as if he were saying: "I am nothing. I will live for you." But each also behaves as if he were saying: "I am nothing, so please live for me."

9. Because they lack trust, certain areas of joint living which especially challenge their ability to take into account the individuality of the other are especially threatening to them. These areas are: money, food, sex, recreation, work, child-rearing, relations with in-laws.

10. Even if they were able to trust others, joint living forces on them decisions about when to give, when to get, within the context of reality at the time. They must decide:

   a. What they will share or do together (how dependent they will be).

   b. What they will not share or do separately (how independent they will be).

11. They must strike some kind of balance within the current reality as to:

   a. What A wants and what B wants.

   b. What A does best and B does best.

   c. What A thinks and what B thinks.

   d. How A will carry responsibilities and how B will carry responsibilities.

12. They need to learn how to assert their thoughts, wishes, feelings and knowledge without destroying, invading or obliterating the other, and while still coming out with a fitting joint outcome.

   a. If they are able to work out a functional relationship, they will say: "I think what I think, feel what I feel, know what I know. I am being *me,* but I do not blame you for being you. I welcome what you have to offer. Let us both see what we can work out that would be most realistic."

   b. But if they are not able to work out a functional relationship, they will say: "Be like me; be one with me. You are bad if you disagree with me. Reality and your different-ness are unimportant."

13. Let us take a trivial example of how "functional" people disagree. Let us say that a couple already understands and accepts the fact that it would be nice to have dinner

together. But we will also say that A wants to go out for a hamburger dinner and B wants to go out for a chicken dinner. The place which serves hamburger does not serve chicken; the place which serves chicken does not serve hamburger.

a.   Each may try to coax: "Please eat hamburgers."

b.   Each may try taking turns: "Let's eat chicken this time and hamburger next time."

c.   They may try to find an alternative which pleases both: "We both like steak so let's eat steak" or "Let's find another restaurant which serves hamburger *and* chicken."

d.   They may take into account a realistic concern which outweighs their separate wishes: "Since the hamburger place is nearer, and we're in a hurry, let's eat hamburger."

e.   They may try to balance their separate wishes against their wish to be together: "You eat hamburger since you like it so much and I will eat chicken, and I will see you later." They are able to separate temporarily and find independent solutions when independence is feasible.

f.   As a last-ditch effort, they may use a third person to make the decision for them: "Charlie wants to eat with us. Let's ask Charlie where he wants to go."

14. Let us take the same example and see how "dysfunctional" people disagree. They operate from the principle that love and total agreement go together. Therefore:

a.   We find them vacillating and postponing: "Let's decide later what to eat" (and they sometimes skip the meal altogether).

b.   We find them trying to coerce: "We are going to eat hamburgers!"

c.   We find them trying to delude each other: "They are both food, so let's eat hamburger."

    d.   We find them trying to undermine each other: "You don't *really* like chicken" or, "you must be crazy to like chicken."

    e.   Always we find them accusing and evaluating morally: "You are bad and selfish for not wanting to eat hamburger. You never do what I want. You have mean intentions toward me."

15. Mary and Joe, to the degree that they are dysfunctional, in effect disagree by saying: "If you loved me you would do what I want." They never use the technique of separating and finding independent solutions; agreed-upon independence is never feasible.

16. Mary and Joe accuse each other because they are disappointed and hurt; they expected total agreement.

    a.   They expected to be valued by the other and they see themselves getting accusations instead.

    b.   They expected to be one with the other and they see themselves getting separation and different-ness instead.

17. Yet if Mary and Joe accuse too openly, several dire results are expected. Joe behaves as if he had said privately to himself:

> "If I accuse Mary, Mary will fall apart. I can't let Mary fall apart because I need her to value me. And suppose Mary refuses to fall apart because she really does not value me? Suppose, instead, that Mary accuses me, hurts me, casts me back into separateness and psychological death, causes *me* to fall apart?"

> "No, that must not happen! Mary needs me. I am responsible for her. I must not accuse Mary or she will fall apart. If I do accuse, I must do it very carefully."

Mary does the same.

18. The disagreement process between Mary and Joe must go underground. (As a matter of fact, most of their communication goes underground, i.e., becomes covert.)

    a.   When Joe and Mary want to accuse each other for not giving, they must hide their accusation and thus communicate covertly.

    b.   When they want to ask for something, they must hide their asking and thus communicate covertly.

19. Here is an example of what covert asking sounds like. Let's say Mary wants to see a movie.

    a.   Instead of Mary saying, "I want to see a movie. Do you?" she may say to Joe, "You would like to see a movie, wouldn't you?" or, "It would do you good to see a movie."

    b.   If she has to hide her request even more (if, for example, she is what we call "schizophrenic"), she may say, "There's a new movie house down the street" or, "I like air conditioning."

20. Here is an example of what covert accusation sounds like Suppose that Joe does not respond to Mary's request.

    a.   Instead of Mary saying, "You don't hear me when I ask for something. You are a schmo!" Mary says, "People never pay attention to me."

    b.   Or, if she has to hide her accusation even more (as with the schizophrenic), she may say, "The world has no ears."

21. When asking and accusing become this hidden, any third person looking on becomes confused and asks: "Who wants what from whom? Who did what to whom?"

    a.   A child in the family can become confused.

    b.   A therapist can become confused unless he sees to it that wishes and accusations get clearly labeled as coming *from* someone and going *toward* someone.

22. As one observes people along the continuum from most functional to least functional, wishes and accusations have fewer and fewer owners.

    a. They become addressed to the nearest planet rather than to the nearest person.

    b. Responses to requests and accusations become increasingly evasive.
        — Messages are sent out as if to no one.
        — Responses are also returned as if to no one.

23. Mary and Joe can evade requests and accusations by withdrawing from the situation. At the same time, they turn their overt withdrawal into a covert accusation.

    a. They may withdraw in so many words: "Do what you like . . . Do it your way . . . You, dear, are always right."

    b. They may withdraw without words by literally leaving the field during crucial decision-making periods, and doing it in such a way that they are covertly saying: "Do what you like. I have to be absent in order to live with you."

    c. They may withdraw through drugs, sleep, alcohol, inattention, "stupidity," in which case they are saying: "Do what you like. I have to be half-conscious in order to live with you."

    d. They may withdraw through physical illness, in which case they are saying: "Do what you like. I have to be sick in order to live with you."

    e. As a last resort, they may withdraw through mental illness, in which case they are saying: "Do what you like. I have to be crazy in order to live with you."

24. Beneath all the evasiveness and ambiguity, Mary and Joe are still trying to solve their conflicting feelings about whether they are loved or unloved.

    a. Each is trying to cover up his disappointment.

b. Each is trying to propitiate, protect, and please the other because he needs the other in order to survive.

c. Whatever they do, the way in which they do it tells how disappointed, martyred, robbed they feel.

25. As a therapist, I have found that the more covertly and indirectly people communicate, the more dysfunctional they are likely to be. However, I have said nothing about the couples who pull and tug in what I call the "teeter-totter syndrome."

a. Each says: "I'm right!" "No, I'm right!" "You are a schmo!" "No, you are a schmo!"

b. Teeter-totter couples at least pull and tug out in the open.
— They do not agree overtly and at the same time disagree covertly.
— One mate does not confuse his own wishes with the other's. Each can hear the other's wishes quite easily because they are usually shouting them.
— Any third person can easily see that these two do not agree and can also comment on this fact and have the comment agreed with.
— The teeter-totter man and wife do not kid themselves, each other, or other people, about how disappointed they feel. However, their individual feelings of low self-esteem create a mutual need for each other and they feel caught. They can acknowledge *different-ness* but not *separateness*.

26. To summarize, Mary and Joe, if they are dysfunctional to an extreme degree (parents of a severely disturbed child), will have low self-esteem, high hopes, and little trust. Thus, they can easily solidify a relationship in which the self and the other become indistinguishable at the surface level. The uniqueness of the self can only be acknowledged covertly.

a. It is as if Joe says to himself: "Mary needs me, I am responsible for her. I must not disagree with Mary, or she will fall apart. Mary and I, we are not different. And we must show no disagreement either except on minor things. She feels what I feel, likes what I like, thinks what I think. We are on the same bloodstream, we live for each other."

    b.   Each tries so hard to please and protect the other that he ends up living by what he thinks the other wants of him.
- Each gives control of himself to the other, while resenting it.
- Each also accepts responsibility for controlling the other, while resenting it.

27. In effect, each ends up acting like a parent one minute and a child the next.

    a.   Each says: "Here, run my life for me (yet I wish you wouldn't!)"

    b.   Each also says: "All right, I will run your life for you (yet I wish you would run your own)."

    c.   Each takes turns at being either the strong, adequate one, or the helpless, inadequate one. There is only room in the relationship for one strong, adequate person.

    d.   Each operates as though being an individual and being a husband or a wife are incompatible; as though individuality and marriage don't go together.

28. Before marriage, Mary and Joe had never thoroughly manifested themselves as individuals.

    a.   Now, after marriage, they try not to show what little individuality they previously manifested, in order to take on the marital role.

    b.   Now, overtly, they try to be just mates living for each other.

    c.   Covertly, they are still trying to exert themselves as individuals.

29. Mary and Joe continue in this kind of relationship because they really expected no other kind.

   a. They can always hope it will be different for them (Life is as life was—but then, maybe it isn't!).
      — Mary can hope that Joe is not what she expected in a man.
      — Joe can hope that Mary is not what he expected in a woman.

   b. Meanwhile, Mary must defend herself against her fears by using the same tactics her parents used against each other because she knows no other kind. (Joe does the same.)

30. Whatever kind of relationship Mary and Joe have worked out, they are disappointed with what they got.

   a. Soon they will be adding the parental role to what is left of their individual roles and to what they have tried to develop as marital roles.

   b. If they found it hard to integrate being an individual with being a mate, they will find it equally hard to integrate being a parent.

CHAPTER IV

Stresses Affecting the Modern Family

1. When Johnny enters the Jones world, his parents'
   expectations and needs are there to greet him.

   a. Johnny, by his very existence, offers Mary and Joe
       another chance to "get," another chance to feel adequate,
       lovable, needed, strong, complete.

   b. Johnny offers his parents a chance to get a true
       extension of themselves, one consisting of their own
       flesh and blood.

2. The trouble is, Johnny has some immediate wants of his
   own.

   a. Right from birth, he makes it clear that *he* is out to get,
       since he is physically helpless and psychologically
       unrelated and unsocialized.

   b. But because he is helpless, his own survival needs must
       be met within the framework of his parents' needs and
       expectations. If he is going to get what he needs, his
       asking must be tuned to what his parents are willing
       and able to give.

3. When Mary and Joe added the parental role to their individual and marital roles, they then qualified, sociologically speaking, as a family. Before discussing the Jones family, it may be profitable to remind ourselves about what sociologists and anthropologists have decided families are, and what functions they perform as a crucial sub-unit of every society.

    a.   They generally seem to agree that the nuclear family (made up of parents and children) is found in all societies.

    b.   They define a family as a group composed of adults of both sexes, two of whom (the mates) live under the same roof and maintain a socially accepted sexual relationship.

    c.   Families also include children created or adopted by these mates.

4. As a social institution, such a group of individuals is held together by mutually-reinforcing functions. These functions are:

    a.   To provide a genital heterosexual experience for the mates.

    b.   To contribute to the continuity of the race by producing and nurturing children.

    c.   To cooperate economically by dividing labors between the adults according to sex, convenience, and precedents, and between adults and children according to the child's age and sex.

    d.   To maintain a boundary (by the incest taboo) between the generations so that smooth task-functioning and stable relationships can be maintained.

    e.   To transmit culture to the children by parental teaching.
       — To teach "roles" or socially accepted ways to act with others in different social situations. (These roles vary according to the age and sex of the child.)
       — To teach the child how to cope with the inanimate environment.

— To teach the child how to communicate; how to use words and gestures so that they will have a generally accepted meaning for others.

— To teach how and when to express emotions, generally guiding the child's emotional reactivity. (The family teaches the child by appealing to his love and to his fear, by communicating to him verbally, nonverbally, and by example.)

f. To recognize when one of its members is no longer a child but has become an adult, capable of performing adult roles and functions.

g. To provide for the eventual care of parents by their children.

5. This is a tall order for families, especially for the mates. Why are mates willing to take on such obligations? Because children are economic assets? Because children are emotional assets? The answer to this question is culturally determined. In our culture, the emotional assets of children predominate.

a. Joe (and the following is true for Mary, too) can feel he has succeeded in fulfilling society's expectations: "Adults bear children. I have a child, too."

b. Joe can gain a feeling of perpetuity by leaving one of his own flesh and blood to live after him.

c. Joe can enjoy over again parts of his own past life by vicariously experiencing his child's discoveries, joys, wonderment.

d. Joe can try to correct for his past pains and mistakes by trying to help his child avoid the avoidable and anticipate future problems.

e. Joe gains added purpose when he notes how very important he is to the child. He must care for, protect, guide, be responsible for his child because he, the father, is obviously the wiser one, the more accomplished one, the authority, the truly stronger one.

f. Joe can feel united with Mary, and Mary can feel united with Joe.

— It took both mates to produce a child; neither could achieve this feat alone.

— It will now take the joint efforts of both to nurture and educate their child. When only one parent is raising a child, that parent has double the work to do and has to make up in some way for the loss of the other parent.

6. But there are deficits to parenting, too, which can fill new parents with conflicting feelings.

    a. Joe and Mary may not have planned to be parents at the time when they actually conceived their child. Perhaps all they thought about were the sexual gratifications they were receiving from each other.

    b. They may have been economically unready to take on responsibilities of feeding, clothing, sheltering.

        — Joe may see the child as demanding an economic support which he feels unable to supply.

        — Mary may have a job which adds to family income (and which she also enjoys), which must now be given up for the sake of the child.

    c. They may be emotionally unready to add a third, dependent member and become a family.

        — Joe may see the child as diminishing Mary's interest in him.

        — Mary may see the child as diverting Joe's interest from her.

        — Mary, who by necessity will take the lion's share of early parenting, may also see the child as a creature who demands all of her and gives little in return, requiring her to isolate herself from adults all day while catering to its needs.

        — Both may be frightened by the total responsibility thrust upon them.

        — Both may wonder, now that the third member creates a family triangle, if someone won't sooner or later get left out.

7. But these are not problems which only Mary and Joe have. All families in the western world have gone through (and

are still reacting to) several material and philosophical influences affecting society as a whole.

8. The Industrial Revolution profoundly affected the modern family, relieving mates of many burdens, yet also placing many extra strains upon them. The effects of this revolution are well known but bear brief repetition here:

   a. It mechanized and de-personalized the work world, leaving the male feeling like a meaningless automaton, laboring at tasks which were only a tiny part of a gigantic, incomprehensible, valueless whole.

   b. It caused individual worth to be rated by income earned, leaving the female feeling down-graded because she did not receive wages for keeping house and rearing children.

   c. Maybe she did not choose to earn her own living, but chose to stay home in the role of wife and mother. If so, she found many family functions taken over by outside institutions: education, food preparation, etc.

   d. The Industrial Revolution emphasized individual mobility as an essential condition of advancement, requiring that whole families follow the money-earner from community to community, leaving old friends behind.

   e. It helped to separate parents from grandparents while failing to replace functions which grandparents previously performed for the nuclear family (such as post-natal home care, babysitting, emergency financial assistance).

   f. The industrial complex made increased specialization in all areas of life mandatory, leaving the individual feeling powerless to influence outer events (local, national, and international). The outside had become a potentially dangerous source of forces which he could barely understand and over which he felt he had no control.

9. Revolutionary intellectual and social influences also affected the modern family by calling into question old assumptions, absolutes, norms, values.

    a. A person's role was no longer something automatic, unquestioned, pre-determined by a static social order and by prearranged manners and customs.

    b. Roles often had to be learned anew for new situations.

    c. Worth had to be earned; it did not come as a birthright. Even if it did come by being earned, it was still uncertainly "relative."

    d. Old patriarchal definitions of the male as the head of the house and the female as belonging in the home went through a re-evaluation. Confused men and women, reacting to the new equalitarian ideals, found themselves questioning and worrying about everyday family tasks and roles.

10. Psychoanalysis, also, profoundly affected concepts about "normal" human behavior, motivation, learning. It led people to reexamine and worry about all aspects of existence, especially about proper child-rearing practices.

    a. The theory implicitly urged parents to give the child freedom to avoid injuring his psychic development.

    b. Over-applied (or carried to a logical conclusion), such ideas immobilized and confused parents. Should they spank or not spank their child? Should they put any restraints on him whatsoever? Family life became increasingly democratic, with children of all ages given a voice and authority about their own upbringing.

11. All these philosophical and economic trends left males and females feeling confused and unimportant.

    a. Men's family lives became so separated from their work lives that they lived almost in two separate worlds.
    — In their work lives, behind a desk shuffling endless papers or behind a machine tightening endless bolts, they felt small, helpless, ignored, insecure.

— Whatever they managed to earn, their families as quickly gobbled up.

— In their home lives they often felt like mother's helper or mother's auxiliary disciplinary force.

— They often wished the family would be geared more to their needs. They were tired and discouraged and rattled from the day's exploits and decisions. They could do with a family turned rest-home or quiet sanitarium.

— Sons, especially, would find an absent, preoccupied, tired, or demoted father an uncertain figure by which to model their lives.

b. Women, living in cities in "boxes in the air" or tucked away in suburbs, felt separated from the bustle and "real purpose" of the modern-day world.

They had been educated for tasks other than housekeeping and child-rearing, and taught to be aware of scientific and cultural events going on outside the family world. They now found themselves losing work experience, seniority, self-confidence, as they focused solely on the wife and mother roles.

— As they focused on housekeeping and child-rearing, society, in turn, took many of their chores away from them or made their household tasks easier and thus more quickly accomplished.

— Some women went outside the home to work, placing their children in nurseries, with neighbors, or with a succession of babysitters. Some stayed home and fretted, parenting in a listless, half-hearted, absent-minded way. Some stayed home and turned child-rearing into an over-intense occupation to compensate for a feeling of uselessness and a feeling that life was passing them by.

12. It is not coincidental that ideas of romantic love and personal happiness became popular in western culture at the same time that old certainties about being a male, being a female, being a person, were shifting and fading.

a. When people felt like "nothing," they were all the more anxious to feel like "everything" to someone.

b. When people could choose a mate to guarantee their personal happiness, and divorce could end the

relationship at will, every married day could become a
shall-we-stay-in-it-or-shall-we-get-out-of-it? day.

c. When people could enter a relationship with a
hypothetical, impermanent attitude, they could become
so busy feeling their pulse for degrees of happiness that
they had little time for enjoying a relationship.

13. Nathan Ackerman, discussing the way wider social
conditions have affected the family, says (20):

The mark of our time is the peculiar disharmony of
the individual's relations with wider society. A
variety of hypotheses come to mind; Durkheim's
concept of anomie, Fromm's emphasis on the trend
to alienation, Riesman's theory of the other-directed
man. Whatever the term, all are agreed on the
trend toward a sense of lostness, aloneness,
confusion of personal identity, and a driven search
for acceptance through conformity. One effect of
this trend toward disorientation is to throw each
person back upon his family group for the
restoration of a sense of security, belongingness,
dignity and worth. The family is called upon to
make up to its individual members in affection and
closeness for the anxiety and distress which is the
result of failure to find a safe place in the wider
world. Individuals pitch themselves back on their
families for reassurance as to their lovableness and
worth. This pressure to compensate individual
members with special security and affection
imposes upon the family an extra psychic load. Is
the contemporary family equipped to carry this
extra load? No—not very well! The family tries, but
it achieves at best a precarious success; often it
fails.

14. Once two World Wars had further disillusioned men and
women, they turned to family-building as a total reason
for being.

a. Child-rearing became a major business and
preoccupation of males and females alike.

   b.   Making children happy became a major theme.

   c.   Giving children what the parents never had became a necessity.

   d.   A child's growth, development, and achievements became a major way for parents to validate their personal worth.

   e.   A child's attitude toward his parents could, to a large extent, make or break their feelings of self-esteem.

15. The parental role took over, as males and females continued to find their relations with each other thorny and threatening.

   a.   Disillusioned with each other, they agreed to "live for the child."

   b.   Yet they implicitly asked that the child live for them; he was the important one, the one who had the power, the responsibility, the mandate to make his parents happy.

CHAPTER V

Marital Disappointment and Its Consequences for the Child

---

1. All modern families go through the stresses and strains of modern society. Yet some manage to produce self-confident children who are capable of coping successfully with a difficult environment.

   a. Sociologists point to delinquent neighborhoods as a major factor in producing delinquency in children. Yet many families live in these neighborhoods and do not produce delinquents, while others in the same neighborhoods produce delinquents in droves.

   b. Psychiatry generally tries to explain these different outcomes by saying that the child who becomes delinquent has a deficiency in psychic functioning: a deficiency in ego development or super-ego controls.

   c. Those of us who have studied family interaction as it affects behavior in children cannot help wondering why the therapy professions have so long overlooked the family as the critical intervening variable between the society and the individual.
      — The family system is the main learning context for individual behavior, thoughts, feelings.
      — *How* parents teach a child is just as important as *what* they teach.

35

— Also, since two parents are teaching the child, we must study family interaction if we are going to understand what the family learning context is like.

2. Family theory postulates that outside forces are important mainly as they affect the parents.

    a. The parents, who teach by words and by demonstration, are the ones who translate to the child the major meaning which outside forces will have to the family.

    b. If the parents, as mates, are disappointed in each other and thus feeling upset, confused, empty, despairing, any outside stress will pack an extra wallop.

    c. If the mates, as individuals, did not integrate what they learned in their own families, they will find it particularly hard to work out a marital integration so that they can give clear, consistent messages to their children.

    d. They will also distort or misinterpret influence from the outside in order to maintain a shaky self-esteem.

3. The marital relationship between Mary and Joe is dysfunctional. As was described, Mary and Joe are low in self-esteem. They looked to each other to enhance self-esteem. But because each saw the other as an extension of self, each failed to give to the other as well as get from the other. So their relationship only increased low feelings of self-esteem. They both became disillusioned and disappointed. The question now remains: How do they fare as parents? To answer this question, one must also ask: How do they see the child? They will see him:

    a. As a vehicle for representing their worth in the community ard for maintaining esteem about self and family.

        "He is the best reader in his class."

        "Everyone says she is the best-behaved child!"

        "We wanted our kid to be what we couldn't be."

b. As a vehicle for maintaining their esteem as people and
    more particularly as parents. They need to feel that the
    child likes them.
    — If, by the child's behavior, he shows that he
      disapproves of them, they are disappointed.
    — This makes it difficult to discipline the child.

c. As an extension of the self.
    — As wanting what they wanted when young. If he
      doesn't want the same things, they are disappointed.
    — As thinking what they think, seeing what they see. If
      he doesn't, they are disappointed.
    — As one to whom everything must be given to make up
      for their own deprivations. If he isn't grateful, they
      are disappointed.
    — As one who will do what they want when they want it.
    — As one who will be a good parent to them.

    "I could hardly wait for her to grow up."

    "I wanted a companion."

    "I hoped that when she grew up we would always
    be close, true friends."

4. But these are wishes which each parent has about the child.
    Trouble arises when each parent comes up against the other
    mate's wishes. The child finds himself caught between
    conflicting demands. Each parent now sees the child as a
    potential:

    a. Ally against the other mate.

    b. Messenger through whom he can communicate with the
        other mate.

    c. Pacifier of the other mate.

5. In other words, each parent's wish for an extension of
    himself gets blocked or challenged by the other parent's
    wishes.

    a. Individual parenting motivations become confused with
        the marital conflict.

b. "Be like me" becomes associated with "Side with me."

c. Both parents battle for preferred place with the child, mainly because neither feels assured of preferred place with the other. (I have often noted the great concern such parents show as to which parent the baby smiled at first.)

6. The trouble is, the child, by virtue of being either a male or a female, already looks like one parent and unlike the other. He is already sexually identified with one parent.

   a. The mates may at first respond to him as a relatively sexless third member of a triangle, and as a vehicle through whom they can express extension-of-self wishes.

   b. But the child does not remain "sexless" very long, as the parents both respond to the fear of being the left out member of a triangle.
— The same-sex parent will see the child as potentially "belonging" more to him.
— The other-sex parent will see the child as potentially becoming like the mate and will fear the child's turning against him. So he will work all the harder to woo the child to his side and to try and make up for deficiencies in the marital relationship.
— As the other-sex parent tries to use the child as an ersatz mate, the child becomes a pawn in a sex war. So the same-sex parent will also tend to see him as a potential competitor. ("He is *like* me but *likes* the other best!")
— This is especially true in dysfunctional families because both mates already feel uncertain about their worth in the eyes of the other and, therefore, extra-fearful about being left out.

7. Given this state of affairs, if the child seems to side with one parent, he runs the risk of losing the other parent. Since he needs both parents, making such a choice inevitably hurts him.

   a. The "left out" parent may retreat from and disparage

both him and the "chosen" parent, and also fail to fulfill basic parenting functions.
— If a boy seems to side with father, mother may say, either overtly or covertly:

> "What can you expect from males!"

> "You're just like your father."

> "What I should have had was a girl."

— If a girl seems to side with mother, father may say, either overtly or covertly:

> "There's women for you!"

> "You're just like your mother."

> "What I should have had was a boy."

— If a boy seems to side with mother, father may say:

> "You and your mother are just alike."

> "Go ahead. Be a mama's boy!"

> "What red-blooded male likes dolls!"

— If a girl seems to side with father, mother may say:

> "You may be smart, but you're going to find it hard with the boys."

> "What girl likes mathematics!"

> "You're your daddy's girl, all right."

(I should add, however, that when a same-sex parent disparages a child for seeming to ally himself with the other-sex parent, he is not just responding from jealousy. He is also trying to help the child develop behavior which seems most appropriate to his sex. He is, in effect, trying to be a good parent.)

b. A child is seriously affected when a parent disparages either him or the other parent *or* when a parent asks him to side against the other parent. In the next chapter

I will discuss the development of sex identity, a development which is made more difficult or is seriously crippled when a parent of either sex includes the child in the marital relationship.

8. In addition to the problem of who will side with whom in the family triangle, we have found that the mates themselves seem to share the same basic conflicts, even though they may often appear at opposite poles in relation to each other.

   a. Each can project his dislike of attitudes or behavior representing one half of the conflict onto the other parent or onto the child, and fight it there.

   b. Or, together, they can fight half of the conflict by inducing the child to act it out and then punishing him when he does.

   c. Or one parent may take one side of the conflict, the other parent the other side, and in this way attack each other through the child.

   d. This is why one must watch how *both* parents behave with each other and with the child.

9. The parents find it least threatening to use the child to "cross monitor" the marital conflicts, that is, to be the vehicle through which hostility can be conveyed indirectly to the other partner.

   a. If the parents show hostility toward each other directly, they run the risk of inviting retaliation. (The child cannot retaliate as successfully.)

   b. If the parents try to express their disappointment in each other by scapegoating the environment, they may lose community approval and risk an attack on their self-esteem.

10. If the mates share the same conflicts but are in constant conflict with each other, parental rules about who a child should be and what he should do cannot help but be

affected. The rules themselves don't jibe with one another, and they are inconsistently enforced.

    a.   An observer of family interaction can come to some fairly reliable conclusions as to what these rules are and how consistent they are, by noting activities which are encouraged, permitted, discouraged, forbidden.

    b.   An observer also notes whether both parents explicitly criticize the child's behavior while at the same time they implicitly encourage it. Both may say, in effect: "Here is your swim suit. Don't go near the water."

11. The child's behavior as he tries to respond to his parent's unlabeled, contradictory wishes reflects and caricatures the unsolved conflicts existing within and between the mates.

    a.   Neither parent, when he uses the child for these ends, is responding to the child as the child is. As Theodore Lidz and his co-researchers note (45):

> Indeed . . . such parents may respond to the child only in terms of their own needs displaced to the child, thus building up an entire pattern of maladaptive interactions.

    b.   Thus the child is unable to distinguish which of his parents' reactions are really about him and which are about one or both of them.

    c.   One might also say that by the time a child has lived long enough in such a learning environment, he does become what the parents see in him. Parental rules about what he should do and be become his rules.

12. The process by which parents induce a child to act out their jointly-held conflicting wishes is, of course, almost entirely unconscious.

    a.   If either parent was aware of how much he influences his child, he would have to be aware of the child as separate from himself.

b. Because of low self-esteem, many parents do not consider themselves as of enough importance to be a factor in influencing a child: "He was born that way."

c. As Jackson puts it (36):

> All of us are only too eager to deny our effect on our children and others around us—just as we have little hesitation in *blaming* the other *guy*. It is small wonder that parents are more intrigued by hereditary and chemical explanations of their child's emotional problems and it thus becomes comes an unpleasant but necessary part of the psychiatrist's job to assess responsibility without laying blame.

13. In general, once parents have focused on a child in a dysfunctional way, they may use him much as a dream symbol is used. Yet, as Bell and Vogel point out, the I. P. symbol is different from a dream-symbol (69):

> While in dreams, any symbolic representation is open to the dreamer, in the family only a very small number of children are available to be used as the potential scapegoats. Hence, when there is a serious . . . problem, and no child is an appropriate symbol of the problem, there must be considerable *cognitive distortion* in order to permit the most appropriate one available to be used as a scapegoat.

14. Once one sees a child being unconsciously used in dysfunctional ways, several questions come to mind:

a. What if there is more than one child in a family? Which child do the mates unconsciously pick to serve the various I. P. purposes?

b. Does the same child continue in the I. P. role all his life, or does another child sometimes take over?

c. Does the sex of the child have anything to do with why one child is assigned the role?

d. Do families exist in which there is more than one I. P.?

e. Each child can be seen as forming the third point in a child-parents triangle. Are children who do not carry out an I. P. function still affected by living in a family which has a dysfunctional child-parents triangle (a triangle which includes in it an I. P.)?

15. We have no research-verified answers as to why marital pairs choose one child as I. P. over another. But from repeated clinical observations we do have some tentative hunches about what leads to the choice. The choice depends, at least in part, on what kinds of conflicts are going on between the mates.

a. Chance characteristics of different children may stimulate conflicts in the mates.
— The child may be ugly, physically deformed, or adopted. Such a child increases parental low self-esteem, and also stimulates whatever ways the mates have of handling what is alien (different-ness). Such a child also threatens the parental need to impress the outside environment because the child may become the object of neighborhood ridicule or curiosity. The parents respond more to protect their self-esteem than to protect the child.
— The child may be especially beautiful or especially intelligent. Such a child may increase parental self-esteem while at the same time lowering it, as the parents contrast themselves with the child.
— The child may look or act like one of his parents or like a grandparent, etc. As Bell and Vogel put it (69):

> In one family, in particular, this pattern was striking. The father and the eldest child had very similar physical characteristics; not only did they have the same first name but both were called by the same diminutive name by the mother . . . The wife's concerns about the husband's occupational inadequacy were not dealt with directly, but the focus for her affect was the child and his school performance.

b. Ordinal position of the child may stimulate conflicts in the mates.
    — One parent may have had problems as the middle child in his own family, and will now focus on his middle child in a special way, fostering sibling rivalry and involving the child in the marital relationship. And, as we so repeatedly note, when one parent has these problems, the other parent also seems to have them.
    — Or the first child may become the I. P. simply because he is available first; he is the first alternative to the mates once marital disappointment sets in.

c. Sex of the child may stimulate conflicts in the mates. Parents may use a child of one sex from birth, or they may use this child only after he or she has gone through growth changes which bring out conflicts between the mates.

d. Age of the child may stimulate conflicts in the mates simply because, as a child grows older, he makes an increasing bid for independence from parental control. A child may not become the I. P. until he reaches the age of adolescent rebellion. If the mates have conflicts about how much independence is allowable in their own relationship, each adolescent child will receive the dysfunctional parental focus.

e. Simple availability of the child can make him the choice for the I. P. role. One child may be in the home when events put an extra strain on the marital relationship. The child away at school may remain free of the dysfunctional focus.

16. In some families the same child remains the I. P. from birth, but in others the role may be shared or passed on from one child to another.

a. In some families all the female children (or all the male children) will, at one time or another, become I. P.'s.

b. In some families each child becomes an I. P. when he reaches adolescence.

c. In some families two or more children carry on the I. P. function simultaneously. Or they take turns. Or one takes one part of the marital conflict and acts it out; another takes the other part.

17. It is also probable that other children are affected by watching the I. P. family triangle in action, even if they, themselves, were never the subject of dysfunctional parental focus.

    a. As I said earlier, if one member of a family has pain which is exhibited in symptoms, all members will, to some degree, react to that pain. They cannot *not* react.

    b. A child learns about people and about himself by interacting with them and by watching them interact. This is why I call any family with an I. P. a dysfunctional family.

18. The next question to ask is: How do the mates unconsciously induce a child to behave in such a way that he eventually gets identified as a "patient"? What does the actual induction process look like and sound like? Here we must take a bypath which leads us into the complex area where communication and symptom development interact.

    a. All of us have had the experience of receiving a double-level message from another person who has not made himself clear (see page 81).
       — If a person's words and expression are disparate, if he says one thing and seems to mean another by his voice or his gestures, he is presenting an *incongruent manifestation,* and the person to whom he is talking receives a double-level message.
       — I call the whole unsatisfactory interaction a "discrepancy," one which can be easily solved if people are able to be explicit.
       — "What did you really mean?" or, "You don't look as if you really meant that," are common statements about discrepancies, and usually the person who is asked the question is able to be explicit, and the double-level message is clarified.*

---

*The whole subject of incongruent communication, focal for this book, will be treated at length in the chapters on communication theory and will be repeatedly

    b.   Thus, by itself, double-level communication need not lead to symptomatic behavior. But under certain conditions, especially where children are involved, it can produce a vice-like situational effect which has been termed the "double bind" (23).

19. What conditions must be present for a child to experience the pressures associated with a double bind?

    a.   First, the child must be exposed to double-level messages repeatedly and over a long period of time.

    b.   Second, these must come from persons who have *survival significance* for him (see pages 45–47).
       — Parents are automatically survival figures because the child literally depends on them for physical life; later, his need for love and approval from them becomes invested with like meaning.
       — In addition, the way the parents structure their messages to the child will determine his techniques for mastering his environment. It is not only his present but his future survival which is in their hands.
       — As a result, he cannot afford to ignore messages from them, no matter how confused.

    c.   Third, perhaps most important of all, he must be conditioned from an early age not to ask, "Did you mean *that* or *that?*" but must accept his parents' conflicting messages in all their impossibility. He must be faced with the hopeless task of translating them into a single way of behaving.

20. Here are a few descriptive examples of the kind of contradictory explicit-implicit messages which help to induce deviant behavior:

referred to in the analysis of family interaction and therapist intervention in Part Three.

a. A mother tells her daughter to be "a little lady." Yet the first gift she sends her at a girl's detention home is a set of seven, sexy, different-colored brassieres.

b. A father says his son shouldn't defy him. Yet he also complains that his son doesn't stand up to him like a man.

c. A mother and father urge their daughter to stay away from wild parties. Yet they allow her to go to such parties. Then, when she calls her father to ask him to bring her home, mother and father kid her about "being scared" in a provoking, demeaning tone.

21. If the parents' messages to a child are consistently like the ones described above, and if he has acquired no means of challenging them, the child is vitally threatened

a. He is threatened in his present dependency because he cannot obey on one level of meaning without disobeying on another, and thus continually invites parental rejection.

b. He is threatened as a future adult because he will take his own ways of dealing with the world from the contradictory and self-deceiving pattern to which his parents have accustomed him.

c. Because the conflict within the messages is hidden and the child has been trained not to "see" it as the source of his disturbance, he turns the blame on himself (in which he is supported by his parents, who can "see" in this matter no better than he can). He says: "I can never do what is right; I must be bad."

d. On the other hand, on a correspondingly covert level, he is quite aware of the impossible situation in which he has been placed. As a last resort, he may answer covertly himself, using the language of disguised protest which society calls "crazy" or "sick" behavior.

22. However, it may take a long time before the child's behavior becomes so exaggerated that it is recognized by society as deviant.

a. We have already spoken of family homeostasis, a process by which the family balances forces within itself to achieve unity and working order.

b. Ways of acting which would not make sense outside the family, like the behavior of a problem child, may be eminently functional within the family, because it allows the marital partners to keep the focus on the child as troublemaker and divert suspicion from the real troublemaker, which is their own conflicted relationship.

c. A child's deviant behavior can thus be functional behavior within a dysfunctional family system. (Therefore, if the therapist understands the perceptions and rules by which the marital partners operate, all behavior in the family makes sense.)

23. Since, to the parents, the existence of the "problem child" is profoundly functional, it is not strange if they are unable to evaluate the degree of his disturbance and should try to protect and perpetuate his behavior. But they walk a very thin line. After all, it is this child who holds the power to make or break the magic circle of family balance and he must be treated carefully as a result.

a. Whichever way he turns, he meets frustration. He can never do what is right because of the contradictory behavior he is asked for, and he can never do what succeeds because he is given such contradictory rules for achieving his goals.

b. If he becomes too upset, he may produce a symptom so eventful that it can no longer be hidden within the family or incorporated into family functioning.

c. So he must be covertly rewarded just enough for his disturbing behavior to offset the official disapproval he earns from it, and to offset his frustration in general. As Bell and Vogel state (69):

> . . . in all instances, while the parents explicitly criticized the child and at times even punished him, they supported in some way, usually implicitly, the persistence of the very behavior

which they criticized. This permission took various forms: failure to follow through on threats, delayed punishment, indifference to and acceptance of the symptom, unusual interest in the child's symptom, or considerable secondary gratification offered the child because of his symptom.

d.   Here we see the suppleness and maneuverability of double-level rule-giving. Not only does it place the child in the position of being "the bad one," "the failure," but it allows for lifting and lightening of its own pressures when they become too much for the child to bear. And all this can be accomplished covertly, beneath the awareness of either the parent or the child.

24.   Thus, the homeostatic system which includes an Identified Patient can remain relatively stable for a long time.

a.   As we have seen, the parents' expectations create a circular interaction. The I. P. acts out the major conflict within and between the parents. When he thus takes on those characteristics which the parents have induced and fear in themselves and in each other, the child becomes the object of their anxiety and makes their expectations come true.

b.   In the following passage, Brodey describes how a child responds to a parent's behavior (27). Here he is talking about the mother-child relationship, leaving out the influence which an ungratifying marital relationship can have on mothering:

> The infant perhaps would learn that survival within this relationship depended on expressing his own needs in a way and at a time conforming with the mother's projected expectation. The long-term reinforcement of the needs which happened to match the mother's, and the frustration of the needs omitted by the mother, would then alter the child's behavior in the direction of validating the mother's projection. Such a relationship between a mother and her internal image of "her child," now projected onto a real child, who actively conforms with this image, gives a realism to the concept of

symbiosis, for the child responded to by the mother is a part of herself.

25. Eventually, even the environment verifies the I. P. label by officially responding to the I. P. as different, delinquent, or sick. It even siphons off the I. P. for special attention and help, as though the problem does mainly center upon him.

   a. Such a labeling and treatment process only helps maintain the system at first, encouraging the parents to rationalize and project even more.

   b. They only increase their focus on the I. P., since they now feel inadequate and fear criticism and blame:

      "He had more than I ever did."

      "He's bad because he wants to be."

      "The school can't handle him either."

      "Young people these days are different."

      "He got in with the wrong gang."

      "He's no member of *this* family!"

   c. The community responds with sympathy to the parents, which only corroborates parental belief that the I. P. is, indeed, someone to be concerned about.

26. But as the community experiences more and more of the child's behavior, it begins to examine parental competence. As the finger of blame is pointed at the parents, the family homeostasis begins to break down or become not worth it. The finger of blame moves from the child to the parents as though it were an either/or proposition.

   a. For one thing, the I. P. victimizes his parents.
      — He calls on them for extra attention or secondary rewards, with his fits, withdrawal periods, runaways, psychotic episodes, etc. This gives him at least the

momentary gratification of being the focus of parental concern.
— He requires special consideration as the sick, different, or bad one. As Murray Bowen says (25):

> The child makes his emotional and verbal demands . . . by exploiting the helpless, pitiful position. Patients are adept at arousing sympathy and overhelpfulness in others. All the research families have eventually found their homes geared to the demands of the patient. The parents are as helpless in taking a stand against the patient as the patient in taking a stand against the parents.

— He manages to get himself exempted from responsibilities, to be relieved from the necessity of dealing with reality beyond the limits which the family sets for him.

b. For another thing, his behavior accentuates the husband-wife conflict.
— Sons get extra attention from mothers, daughters from fathers. So the basic dynamics of the family triangle become exacerbated.
— The mates end up blaming each other. As Bell and Vogel put it (69), the parents privately consider themselves at least partly responsible for the child:

> Thus, the child's disturbance feeds back into the problems which must be faced by the parents, and the marital pair often project the responsibility for the child's disturbance onto each other.

c. Eventually, perhaps, the community takes the I. P. away from the family or recommends/insists on therapy for the family. This challenges the homeostatic balance and also the parents' adequacy as parents. As Haley says (about a psychotic I. P.) (33):

> Although psychotic behavior may serve a function in a family system, a risk is also involved. The patient may need to be separated from the family by hospitalization and so break up the system, or he may enter therapy and change and so leave the system. Typically, the parents seem to welcome hospitalization only if the patient is still accessible to them, and they welcome therapy for the patient

up to the point when he begins to change and
infringe the rules of the family.

27. In every respect, a marital relationship which requires an
Identified Patient can do nothing but bring disappointment,
destructiveness and pain to all three persons.

   a. Parental hopes to please and impress the community by
   having a child who represents the family's ideals can be
   shattered overnight by I. P. behavior.

   b. A parent's hopes that his child will like him can be
   shattered overnight by I. P. anger and rebellion.

   c. Hopes that the child will fulfill a parent's own ambitions
   can be shattered when an I. P. quits school or gets
   himself expelled.

   d. Hopes that a child will help bring the parents closer
   together can be shattered when I. P. behavior ends up
   accentuating marital difficulties.

   e. In every way, unsolved marital conflicts boomerang on
   the mates as they valiantly try to be good parents. And
   such conflicts cannot help but affect the whole family.
   As Lidz dramatically describes it (44):

   > . . . these marriages . . . indicate the virtual absence
   > of complementarity. . . . Husband and wife do not
   > support each other's needs and the marital
   > interaction increases the emotional problems of
   > both, deprives the spouses of any sense of
   > fulfillment in life, and deteriorates into a hostile
   > encounter in which both are losers. Instead of any
   > reciprocal give and take, there is demand and
   > defiance leading to schism between partners that
   > divides the entire family, leaving the children torn
   > between conflicting attachments and loyalties.

28. The Identified Patient, however, suffers the most, in spite of
receiving occasional relief from the role, or occasional
secondary rewards.

a. He internalizes the marital conflicts, which makes it difficult for him to maintain gratifying male-female relationships. He continues to live out the family drama with other males and females, and long after the other two participants in the drama are dead.

b. He feels low self-esteem. His label as the bad, different, or sick one only reinforces his belief in his own worthlessness.

c. He is inappropriately trained to cope outside the family. As Lidz says about the family of the schizophrenic (45):

> The world as the child should come to perceive it is denied. Their [parents'] conceptualizations of the environment are neither instrumental in affording consistent understanding and mastery of events, feelings, or persons, nor in line with what persons in other families experience. Facts are consistently being altered to suit emotionally determined needs. The acceptance of mutually contradictory experiences requires paralogical thinking. The environment affords training in irrationality.

29. Here is a brief excerpt from a family therapy session which helps show how conflict between the husband and wife produces symptomatic behavior in the child.

a. In this excerpt, the induction process is demonstrated indirectly through the conversation of the mates.

b. This marital pair is well on its way to seeing how the marital conflict affects the child.

c. They are also able to discuss the marital relationship as relatively separate from the child. (This contrasts markedly with the inability of parents of a schizophrenic child to discuss their relationship as such.)

d. Once the family therapist can help the mates deal with each other in a more gratifying way, he helps free them to see the child as the child is. Gratifications will then follow for both the child and the parents, since children desperately want to please their parents, and parents basically want to do well by their child.

Excerpt:

W: With the children I have to put them on a double standard too.

Th: Well, why?

W: Well, because my husband can do things, lose his temper and things like that where they're not allowed to. I mean he can pinch and poke them sometimes where they're not allowed to pinch and poke each other when they're irritable.

Th: This obviously introduces a problem which I think . . .

W: I mean, how can I tell Harry, or sometimes George, not to pinch, not to poke, when my husband does it to Harry?

Th: How do you handle it?

W: Some days I don't. But I prod my husband on these points where he'll, where he would lose his temper, but because I'm prodding him he won't lose his temper and I know that. But still I feel that in not losing his temper that he is getting self-restraint where at one time he would have lost his temper on the same thing without my actually wanting him to really get angry, but still, I . . .

Th: You want to pay your husband back.

H: That's what she wants to do.

W: I like to see him, uh . . .

H: That's what she wants to do.

W: I like to see him, I want to see him hold restraint. I like, uh, I don't . . .

Th: I would think you'd want to pay him back.

H: That's what she does.

W: I do that quite often, too.

Th: Sure, all right, so we look at it. He provokes you; you want to pay him back. You provoke him; he wants to pay you back. I think that's kind of what we've been seeing here, one way or the other, for reasons you haven't understood, but I think this has been going on here. (pause) I don't think you have understood it.

H: See, you're, I mean I feel there's, there's, in other words you're saying that the irritation I've felt about our relationship I've taken out on Harry?

Th: Uh hm. Without meaning to. He's the battleground for both of you.

H: Well you're right and I agree. I've felt this a long time.

30. The induction process, as I have described it, may seem to some readers entirely too one-sided.

   a. What part does the child play in all this? Or are children simply blank sheets upon which their parents write?

   b. Doesn't a child have a choice about accepting or not accepting an I. P. role?

   c. To help answer these questions one must also ask another: What do all children need from their families if they are going to grow up to be functional adults?

   d. In the next chapter we will try to look at the world, not as adults see it, but from a child's point of view.

CHAPTER VI

What All Children Need in Order to Have Self-Esteem

1. I have been describing marital dysfunction as it affects the parenting of at least one child in a family, the child who becomes an Identified Patient.

    a. If the mates have low self-esteem and little trust in each other, they will expect their child to enhance their self-esteem, to be an extension of themselves, and to serve crucial pain-relieving functions in the marital relationship.

    b. But this sounds entirely too one-sided, as though a child has no choice but to accept the role his parents are asking him to play, or as though children are simply blank sheets upon which their parents write.
       — Children are not just blank sheets. They come into the world with distinct constitutional differences. (Simply in terms of "body reactivity," newborn infants are markedly different.) They also come into the world as either biological males or biological females.
       — Yet all children come into the world helpless. Whatever they require for survival must be given to them or taught to them. No child comes into this world with a blueprint of what he shall do and be. This can only come from the people with whom he lives, and whom I call survival figures for this reason.

2. From birth, for example, a child needs to be physically comfortable. He needs to be fed and warm so that the transition from womb to home is as smooth as possible.

3. From birth, a child also needs continuity in relationships.

   a. When food and warmth come, he needs to have the same person bringing them, touching him, and talking to him.

   b. He needs to have the same human voice and touch introduce him to the existence and predictability of one "other."

   c. Even when he is fed and warm, he learns to require the physical presence of mother; he learns to require relationship *per se.*

4. A child needs to learn how to influence and predict the responses of others.

   a. As he learns how to differentiate mother from all others, he also learns to develop different mother-influencing responses.
      — When he cries, food, warmth, and body contact usually come. Yet sometimes they don't come.
      — Some special kinds of cries work better than others at bringing mother.
      — Smiles bring extra-special treatment from mother.

   b. When he learns to include father as a survival figure, he will also develop special father-influencing responses.

5. A child needs to learn how to structure the world.

   a. With the help of language, he learns how to differentiate and classify beyond the world of self, father, and mother. He learns to classify cats and dogs, adults and children, males and females, family and not-family.

   b. From his parents he learns not only how to classify but how to evaluate and predict. He learns to differentiate

between "good" and "bad" feelings, good and bad
behavior, etc.

6. A child needs to esteem himself in two areas: as a masterful
person and as a sexual person.* He will develop esteem
about himself as a masterful person (a person able to do for
himself) if at least one parent validates his developmental
growth.

   a. A parent validates this growth when he (or she):
      — Notes the existence of growth.
      — Communicates verbally or non-verbally that he
        notices.
      — Gives the child increased opportunity to manifest and
        exercise the new abilities emerging from growth.

   b. As the child grows and learns, he becomes increasingly
      able to do more things for himself, to take care of
      himself.
      — He can feed himself, go to the toilet by himself, tie his
        own shoes, anticipate and avoid dangerous objects; in
        other words, he can handle his own body in relation to
        the environment and he can manipulate objects.
      — Mastery grows to include the ability to make
        decisions, to reason, to create, to form and maintain
        relationships, to time needs in relation to reality, to
        plan ahead, to tolerate failure and disappointment.

   c. To validate a child's mastery, parents must be able to
      recognize when a developmental stage has been reached
      and so appropriately time the validation.
      — They must not expect the child to be five when he is
        eight, or eight when he is five.

---

*I have chosen to separate esteem as a masterful person from esteem as a sexual
person for two reasons. First, there are certain abilities and activities which are
not necessarily linked with a person's sex. Both males and females learn to work,
think, read, problem-solve, experiment. (Of course, because these capacities are
shared, they also serve to enrich male-female relationships.) Second, I have noted
how some people can have esteem in one area of identity and not in the other.
Adults may be able to relate sexually to the other sex but be unable to master
themselves or the environment, and vice versa.

— In other words, for validation to be validation, it must fit the needs, abilities, and readiness of the child. And the acknowledgement of this validation must be clear, direct, and specific.

d. Parental validation does not imply uncritical approval of everything a child wishes to do. Parents are the socializers; they must teach the child that he is not the center of their world or of the world at large.
    — He must learn how to fit in with the requirements of family living, how to balance his needs with those of others, how to fit into the demands of the culture.
    — He needs to develop skills for coping with and balancing the requirements of *you, me* and *the context,* at this point in time, under these circumstances.
    — He may scream and complain at restrictions or rules, but accepting restrictions and learning rules is part of growing up. "Restrictions" and "validation" are not opposing terms.
    — Nor does parental validation mean intense, over-solicitous attention to a child's every need. Parents are people, too. Johnny may be ready to walk, with mother's encouragement, but mother, at the moment, may be busy at the stove.
    — Parental validation is most effective when it is administered in a relatively matter-of-fact way.

e. If a parent does not validate a child's ability, or inappropriately times his validation, the child has trouble integrating the ability. It remains a fragmented aspect of the "unimportant me" or the "inadequate me" or the "secret me." Parents may:
    — Fail to see abilities when they are obvious, or give no opportunity for their expression, or show no approval or disapproval when the child manifests them.
    — See abilities prematurely and anxiously urge their expression.
    — See abilities incorrectly (abilities which are simply not there) and anxiously urge their expression.
    — See abilities but discourage and punish their expression.

f. If, when one parent validates a child's abilities, the other parent contradicts the validation, the child's learning

will be more difficult and he will manifest what he
knows in a more inconsistent way.
— One parent may expect much from the child, the
  other parent, little.
— So a family therapist must be alert to how *both*
  parents go about validating each ability in a child.

g. If parents do not validate an ability (if they do not see it,
    or if they punish it), the child will still continue to grow,
    since all life is geared toward continuous growth.
    However:
    — He may not allow himself to manifest the ability.
    — He may manifest it secretly.
    — He may manifest it in a distorted or disguised fashion.
    — In any case, the ability will not contribute to his
      self-esteem.

7. A child will develop esteem about himself as a sexual person
    only if both parents validate his sexuality.

a. He must identify with his own sex, yet that very
    identification must include an acceptance of the other
    sex.
    — Males validate females as females, females validate
      males as males.
    — Identification, in this sense, is a two-sided affair: "I
      am a male in relation to females. It is good to be a
      male because of what females are."

b. Sexual identification is the result of a three-person
    learning system. Parents validate a child's sexuality by
    how they treat him as a small sexual person. But they
    mainly validate it by serving as models of a functional,
    gratifying male-female relationship.
    — The context for learning to esteem one's sexuality can
      be diagrammed like this:

        Father (big male)——————Mother (big female)

                A   B   C

                    child (little male)

— A and C are both interactions. B represents the demonstration by husband and wife (as observed by the boy) of adult male-female relations. The demonstration carries the greater weight. (Note that I specify that the child is a little male and his parents are a big male and a big female.)

c. Many people, when they think of families, think of them merely as small groups made up of individuals performing similar or interchangeable role-functions.
   — Family members are not sexless, ageless bodies interacting. They are adult males and females interacting with little males and females.
   — The whole world is made up of males and females. The most psychologically influential roles people play are sex-linked roles. Males are somebody's son, somebody's brother, somebody's boyfriend, somebody's husband, somebody's father, etc. Females are somebody's daughter, etc.
   — Males and females also fill roles which are not sex-linked, such as somebody's boss, somebody's teacher. But usually the sex of that boss or teacher carries special meaning derived from earlier relationships which were sex-linked.

d. If a child needs both sex models, what happens if a boy's father dies when he is born and his mother doesn't remarry? Does this mean that the boy will not develop an esteem about himself as a male person?
   — No, because children are ingenious at creating from the wider environment whatever is missing in family life. They use uncles, grandfathers, older brothers, neighbors, teachers, any available older male.
   — Even children in orphanages make models out of older boys and girls, or out of the housemother and the janitor.
   — Children will also make up a picture of what father was like from all the bits and pieces of data about father which they can receive from mother, grandmother, grandfather, etc.
   — The child will be able to use male models if he receives a message from mother that males are valuable. If he receives a message that males are not valuable and that it hurts mother when he reaches out for models, then he will use available models covertly and in a distorted way.

8. When the parents are not able to validate each other as sexual people, they will not be able to validate the child as a sexual person either.

   a. Overt or covert disparagement will be going on between them and they will not provide models of a functional, gratifying, male-female relationship.

   b. Moreover, if they are in conflict with each other they will be in conflict with the child, too. He will thus receive contradictory messages from them as to what he should do and be. He will be asked to go north and south at the same time.

   c. Also, the parents will use the child as a pawn in the marital conflict. They will ask him to take sides in it. He will often find himself alternately disparaged by one and validated by the other.

   d. All in all, he will be subjected to highly contradictory or discrepant experiences.

9. To illustrate, let us break down family interaction into a series of questions which a male child may be said to ask himself. The answers to these questions will form the basis for his sexual identification.

   a. How does father (big male) treat mother (big female)?
      How does father treat me (little male)?
      How does father tell me to treat mother?
      How does mother (big female) treat father (big male)?
      How does mother treat me (little male)?
      How does mother tell me to treat father?

   b. I will try to show, under each question, some very simple kinds of contradictions which may be presented to a child.

10. How does mother treat me?
    How does father treat me?

    a. The child asks himself, in effect: How does mother (or father) react to the fact that I have genitals, that I manifest sexual feelings (in masturbation, nocturnal emissions, erections, etc.), that I manifest sexuality toward others (in sex play, kissing, petting, and later on, in intercourse)? How does mother (or father) react to my interest in toys, my choice of clothes, my fights with boys?

b. This the child can size up for himself because it is a matter of fairly direct experience.
   — He listens to what each says to him. Mother may tell him it is not natural to masturbate. Father may tell him there is no harm in it.
   — He listens to what each says about him to the other. Father may say, "Johnny is a weakling." Mother may say, "He is not. He is just a boy."
   — He notes how each behaves with him. Father may laugh when he "plays the field" with the girls. Mother may scold him for kissing *any* girl.
   — He notes how each reacts to the other's behavior with him. Father may spank him when he stays out late. Mother may then scold father for being too strict.
   — He notes how each tells him to behave and how they themselves behave. Father may tell him not to steal, yet proudly cheat on his income tax. Mother may tell him not to lie, yet allow him to pass for twelve instead of fourteen when he goes to the movies.

c. We must further keep in mind the fact that most children have the experience of being in the presence of both parents. Thus the opportunities for inconsistency are multiplied.

11. How do mother and father treat each other?

a. Here the boy does not always have direct experience to go by.
   — How mother and father treat each other includes how they engage in sexual intercourse. This is usually not observed by the boy unless he has a chance to do "keyhole" research.*

---

*Adults, in our culture, do not openly demonstrate their sexuality before children, they just give occasional hints about it in jokes, embraces, kisses, etc. I am not recommending that they demonstrate it, either. But it is interesting to note how Eskimo children, for example, do not seem to suffer from frequent demonstrations of their parents' sexuality.

— Even if the boy does chance to observe his parents in intercourse, he is not apt to understand the act in its adult meaning; to him it looks as if father is hurting mother. This would then be data about hurting rather than loving.

b. All that the child can observe directly is how his parents seem to get along with each other day by day. This, too, may be confusing.
— He may see them fight during the day, yet sleep in the same bed at night.
— He may hear them complain about "apron strings" or "balls-and-chains," yet see that each one grieves when the other is away.
— He may not see them fight openly, yet still observe from their behavior that they are tense and angry with one another.
— He may see them looking as though perennially hurt and not know what the hurt is about

c. To add to the possible confusion, he must integrate how they treat each other with how they treat him.
Consciously or unconsciously he must figure out:
— How come mother lets him know when she is hurt or sad, yet never lets on to father?
— How come father lets him have anything he wants, yet gripes whenever mother buys a new dress?
— How come mother urges him to be the toughest male on the block, yet insists that father keep his temper?

12. How does mother tell me to treat father?
How does father tell me to treat mother?

a. The child asks: Does mother disparage father, but tell me to treat him with respect? Does father beat up mother, but tell me to treat her with respect?

b. Many of these contradictory experiences could and would be explained in a functional family because the child could ask about them. The child could then learn that each experience has its own set of variables and is not necessarily linked to a similar one.

c. In a dysfunctional family, children get the impression that they may not ask questions. Questions might lead to

discussions of the marital relationship, and the mates
are too pained about that to be able to discuss it openly.

13. When the child is thus left with unexplained contradictions,
he will try to explain them to himself, often coming up with
incomplete or incorrect conclusions.

    a.   In order to come to conclusions, he may dangerously
distort or ruthlessly discard the facts of his experience.

    b.   For example, he may decide about the male-female
relationship that:
— If someone is "hurt," the other "inflicts hurt."
— If someone is "weak," the other is "strong."
— If someone "loses," the other "wins."
— If someone is "good," the other is "bad."

    c.   Such overly simple black-and-white conclusions make
integration of models especially difficult and seriously
hamper the development of self-esteem. For example:
— The boy can try to reject one parent (which we will
call "north") and choose the other parent ("south"). In
so doing, he fails to include one sex as a model. Since
he *cannot* unambivalently make such a choice, his
rejection of one sex must remain incomplete.
— He can try to reject both north and south. In so doing,
he fails to include either sex as models. He refuses to
integrate males in relation to females and females in
relation to males, but such a refusal is also
incomplete.
— He can try to integrate what cannot be integrated by
trying to go north and south at the same time. In so
doing, he remains immobilized in his efforts to use
either sex model.

    d.   A boy's esteem about himself as a male will suffer most
if his father looks the most hurt, disparaged, or
depreciated in the marital relationship. A girl's esteem
will suffer if it is her mother who looks the most hurt.
— This may be why we so often see sex-linked pathology
in families where all the males or all the females
manifest pain overtly in symptoms. (Of course, the
other children in such families are also feeling pain,

even though their pain may not be labeled as pathological.)

— Since children readily tend to identify with the parent of the same sex (identify in the sense of seeing themselves as genitally like one and unlike the other), it is frightening to see the same-sex parent either inflicting hurt or being hurt.

— Of the two, however, the thought of being hurt is the more frightening. ("This will happen to me, too!")

— In spite of other characteristics which stimulate the tendency to see oneself as more like one parent than the other, genital similarity carries with it similar destiny in relation to the other sex.

14. If parents consistently show that they consider their child a masterful, sexual person, and if they also demonstrate a gratifying, functional male-female relationship, the child acquires self-esteem and becomes increasingly independent of his parents.

 a. When the time comes for him to partly leave home to attend school, he is confident about doing so (and encouraged to do so by his parents). He is able to profit from substitute parent figures (teachers) for much of his remaining education.

 b. Also, as he grows in sexual maturity, he is able to turn away from the family, seek a sexual partner for himself, and set up his own independent life.

 c. In choosing a partner, he does not (as Mary and Joe did) seek someone with whom he feels safe or who will bolster his self-esteem. Because he already esteems himself, he is relatively independent of what others think of him (including his mate). So he can take the individuality of his mate into account without requiring, for his own safety, that the mate be an extension of him.

 d. In every way, self-esteem, independence and individual uniqueness go together.

15. The close relationship between parental validation, self-esteem, independence, and uniqueness shows up when

one observes how a dysfunctional person (an unvalidated child who is now an adult) still clings to his parents, or to substitute parent figures, or relates to his sexual partner as if that partner were, in fact, a parent.

    a.   Such an adult remains in the parental home long after he is physically grown.

    b.   Or he continues to be closely involved in his parents' lives. He moves back in with them later in life. Or he allows them to move in with him. Or he lives around the corner from them and sees them so frequently that it is often difficult to distinguish between his home and theirs.

    c.   Or he leaves his parents but continues to seek validation from substitute parent-figures outside the home (from an employer, older friend, etc.). He may label one such figure a "mate" and marry her, but relate to her as to a parent.

16. Does this mean that when we see parents who have failed to validate their children we can assume they did not want their children to become independent of them? This is partly so, but is too simple a way to explain the complex motivations involved in dysfunctional parenting.

    a.   Parents who fail to validate their children are usually to disappointed in their marital relationship and too involved in filling their own needs even to see their children as individuals, much less see their needs. They are themselves products of dysfunctional parenting.

    b.   Their failure to validate is more an act of omission than of commission. They desperately wish to be good parents.

    c.   Because dysfunctional parents see "parenting" as uninfluenced by their own pained marital relationship, they are unaware of the fact that what they build with one hand they tear down with the other.

CHAPTER VII

The Family Triangle
A Brief Aside

1. We need to take some time out, before going on to the
    chapters on communication, to evaluate certain family
    behavior which seems to contradict the thesis that a child
    needs his parents to have a functional, gratifying
    relationship and will automatically thrive if they do
    have one.

    a. Transcribed excerpts of early family therapy sessions
        show that:
        — When husband and wife start to argue, the I.P.
        intervenes and diverts their focus onto himself.
        — In the same way, when husband and wife start to get
        together amicably, the I. P. intervenes and diverts
        their focus onto himself.

    b. Many psychologists have seen this behavior as
        emanating from a child's sexual wishes for the other-sex
        parent. This wish continually leads him to try to
        separate his parents while at the same time it leads him
        to bring them together, partly because he fears
        castration and partly because he needs them both.

2. My own interpretation is somewhat different. To begin with,
    I do not postulate sex as the basic drive of man. From what I

have observed, the sex drive is continually subordinated to and used for the purpose of enhancing self-esteem and defending against threats to self-esteem.

   a. It is true that two people who have high self-esteem, and who openly behave in accordance with their own uniqueness, will come out as sexually identified, masterful, creative people.

   b. However, the need to feel esteem about the self is so important that adult mates will do without sexual satisfaction or fail to demand it in a vital relationship if sexual behavior or demands for it lead to threatened self-esteem. One sees this over and over again when counseling marital pairs.

   c. The need for sexual satisfaction continues to exacerbate problems in the marital relationship, but the mates continue in the relationship nonetheless; the need to protect self-esteem, as demonstrated by such marital solutions, takes precedence over the sexual need.

3. I explain the I. P.'s behavior in therapy as follows:

   a. When the boy's parents argue, the boy fears that one or both of them may be destroyed in the process.
      — He does not want to lose either parent; he loves and needs them both.
      — He has learned that when he diverts their focus onto himself, his parents stop arguing.

   b. When, in family therapy, the boy's parents start to get together amicably, he is presented with an entirely new situation.
      — A boy in a dysfunctional family has never had the experience of united parents. When they tried to appear united, he always knew that they were not. Now, when they might actually be taking their first steps toward amicability, he has no experience by which to evaluate their behavior.
      — Also, up to now his own needs have been met only through their needs. If his parents get together, they may ignore him altogether; he may be abandoned. He has never had the experience of being left out of the

marital relationship yet still assured of appropriate parenting.

— Although his present role as I.P. is a burdensome one, he knows no other family role and, like his parents, he fears change. Both he and his parents actively cooperate to keep family therapy parent-child focused.

c. I have been repeatedly struck by how readily the I.P. drops his role as intervener once family therapy is under way. Once he is assured that arguments do not bring destruction and that marital amicability lightens parental demands on him, the I.P. actively helps the therapist help his parents *as mates,* while at the same time he tries to get his parents to recognize him as a separate individual with needs of his own. As a matter of fact, the I.P. is often very helpful as "assistant marital counselor."

4. The question may still be asked, though: Why do we see over-developed father-daughter, mother-son relationships repeatedly showing up in dysfunctional families?

a. Doesn't this prove that each child really parents; that he not only sets out to do so but, in a sense, succeeds? And that when he thinks he has succeeded, he manifests symptoms?

b. Symptoms may, to some degree, originate from the Oedipal conflict. But my question is: How did this conflict come about?

5. I believe that the Oedipal development only becomes an Oedipal "conflict" when the individual is unable to integrate an appropriate picture of his own sex with a compatible picture of the other sex. Whether this happens or not depends on whether the parents are clear, direct and specific in relation to their different-ness and uniqueness.

a. Children are born with the ability to express feelings about their sexuality toward anyone without guilt.

b. But children are born into a world which imposes strict taboos on certain expressions and behavior in regard to sexuality. The most important of these is the incest taboo, imposed to protect the child and to protect the adult sexual relationship.

    c.   Children learn that the incest taboo exists when they express their feelings toward the other-sex parent and receive disapproval which induces guilt and fear, threatening their self-esteem.

6. But guilt and fear alone do not lead to a crippling Oedipal development.

    a.   Children in functional families receive clear, consistent admonishments that neither parent is a suitable object for the child's increasingly strong sexual feelings.

    b.   The child of such parents will be "conflicted" by such admonishments to the same degree that he is conflicted by any restraints put on his endless self-wishes.

    c.   The child's sexual feelings, *per se,* are not frowned on. He is assured that such feelings only require expression elsewhere.

7. The incest taboo becomes something to be strongly conflicted about when both parents enforce it inconsistently and one parent positively encourages the child to try and break it.

    a.   In dysfunctional families, the other-sex parent fosters incestuous feelings by overtly expressed expectations and demands.

    b.   The same-sex parent fosters guilt about such feelings when he fails to intervene with the mate and with the child, yet at the same time disparages and withdraws from the child, causing the child to drift all the more toward the seductive parent.

    c.   The incest taboo, by itself, causes only minor conflict in the child. It is the parents' inconsistency about the taboo which both stimulates sexual feelings and increases guilt.

8. As I said before, in any triangle, all three members can have fears about being left out.

   a. In my opinion there is no such thing as a relationship between three people. There are only shifting two-person relationships with the third member in the role of observer.

   b. In a family triangle, the wife fears that her husband will be less interested in her, the husband fears that his wife will be less interested in him, and the child (when he becomes aware of his father) fears that he will not be the center of his parents' world.

   c. By age two a child is definitely aware of his father as a person who is gone all day but who comes home at night, demanding attention from his wife.
      — Children of both sexes respond to the arrival of father with interest and fear. They must now figure out where they fit with two significant others.
      — A child tries to solve the dilemma either by running from one to the other, or by getting both, as a unit, to concentrate on him.

9. In the functional family triangle, the mates are confident about their own marital relationship and so are able, in an unthreatened way, to handle the child's fears of being left out.

   a. Mother is able to allow the child a father-child relationship.

   b. Father is able to allow the child a mother-child relationship.

   c. Yet both mates make it clear to the child that he can never be included in their relationship as mates.

10. In the dysfunctional family triangle, the mates are not confident about their own marital relationship.

    a. They already feel left out with each other. (As a matter of fact, one of the principles from which all members in such a family operate is: There is not enough to go around. Who is going to get what is available?) Both mates look to the child to satisfy their unmet needs in the marital relationship.

— Because they are disappointed in each other and engaged in a marital war, they both ask the child to side with them. (This means siding against the other parent.)
— The mother, in her efforts to turn the boy child into an ally and ersatz mate, also woos him seductively, offering him an added inducement. (A father will do the same with his daughter.)
— The boy, being a sexual person, will respond to his mother's affection in kind. He will do so without any feeling of guilt at first; his mother's behavior will simply look like approval behavior: "She likes me."
— The father reacts to the close mother-son relationship with disapproval, disparagement and withdrawal. The boy receives the message: "Father doesn't like me."
— And when the boy notes how mother disparages her mate at the same time that she approves of him, he receives another message: "Mother likes me better than father."
— The boy loves and needs both of his parents. He can only feel conflicted by his mother's love: "Mother's love loses me Father."

b. Incest terrors show themselves, in reality, as learned responses to an actual environment.
— Mother does show jealousy toward Johnny when Johnny seems to side with father.
— Father does show jealousy toward Johnny when mother invites Johnny to become ersatz mate and ally.
— Yet both parents allow Johnny to think that he is essential to their marital relationship. When he tries to avoid taking sides or avoid being used in their sex war, they both continue to involve him.
— As for Johnny's castration fears, he has good reason to worry about losing his penis. Since females don't have one, the penis does come to look like something that could be taken away by an angry person. (And, more often than not, he receives just such threats, overtly or covertly, from either or both parents.)

11. I should add that although a son may appear closer to and allied with his mother (as a daughter may appear closer to and allied with her father) such an alliance is illusory.

   a. Such a relationship may be interpreted by mother and father as siding, but it is not siding as far as the boy is concerned.

   b. Children cannot unambivalently side with either parent.

   c. Children long for and need an accepted relationship with each parent. This is one of the ways their mastery and sexuality gets validated.

   d. Another way is by example. A mother does not have to engage in sexual intercourse or in seductiveness with her boy in order to assure him of his worth as a male. She indirectly validates him by engaging in intercourse with her husband and by openly enjoying and approving of her husband as a male person. She also validates her son by letting him know that she approves of his sexuality and of his eventually seeking a sexual partner of his own.

12. Because both mates in a dysfunctional family are particularly sensitive about being left out, the child does, in effect, end up by losing one parent unless he is able to reassure both parents by walking the precarious tightrope between them.

   a. The son ends up with a distant relationship to father.

   b. The daughter ends up with a distant relationship to mother.

13. A child who becomes an Identified Patient in a dysfunctional family is saddled with far more than incestuous desires and castration fears.

   a. He is saddled with the burden of believing that he actually does hold his parents together. He learns that he can unite them in some fashion at least by getting them to focus on him.

— This happens naturally, as he ricochets from one
parent's extension-of-self wishes to the other's.
— This also happens as he tries to get validation of
himself as an individual with needs of his own and
these efforts are perceived as rebellious, unloving
behavior.
— Since he cannot please both of his parents and also
himself, he manifests increasingly contradictory and
extravagant behavior.
— Such bad, different, crazy or sick behavior leads his
parents to unite all the more in an intense focus
on him.

b. But such a way of uniting his parents does not really
relieve marital pain, nor does it ever really include the
I. P. in the marital relationship. He suffers from a
burdensome delusion that he is an "insider." (In a
functional family, such a delusion would, as a matter of
course, be dispelled.)
— The I. P. does not stop his parents' pain. All he does is
divert the expression of it onto himself.
— He is not a genuine part of the marital relationship.
That relationship is a closed system, physically and
psychologically. The child is littler than his parents
are, he doesn't know what they know, he cannot do
what they can do. In no way can he relate to either of
them as they can relate to each other. He is not their
equal, sexually or otherwise.
— Even as an "outsider," the I. P. lacks experience or
judgment as to what the pain is all about, so that
whatever he does to relieve pain is bound to be
unfitting and unsuccessful. (For example, adults may
manifest their pain in different ways. Father may
show his pain by bullying behavior with mother.
Mother may show her pain by crying. To a child,
mother thus looks more pained in the marital
relationship than father does. How can he fully
understand their mutual pain when he sees his
parents through such a simple lens?)

c. Even though the I. P. cannot relieve pain, his parents
allow him to believe that he can, and that he is essential
to the marital relationship. So he suffers from another
burdensome delusion: that he is omnipotent.
— Why would they both respond so intently to him if he
were not very important?

— Why would they both ask him to side with them if he were not equal to them?

— Why would they both rely on him to validate their self-esteem and represent the family in the community if he were not all-powerful.

— Why would they rely on him to hold their marital relationship together if he were not a part of it?

— Who but an omnipotent, omniscient King would be treated in such ways?

d. The I. P. is, in effect, burdened with the responsibility of living for his parents. His own needs are ignored and he has never discovered a way of getting them attended to.

— As a result, he swings from omnipotence to helplessness, from grandiosity to self-abnegation.

— He develops little ability to predict in relationships.

— And, because his needs remain unvalidated, he is distrustful of others, yet dependent to a crippling degree on what others think of him.

CHAPTER VIII

Communication:
A Process of Giving and Getting Information

1. What do we mean by "communication"? Isn't studying how people communicate almost like studying how they walk across a room? Doesn't this amount to ignoring the deeper processes which psychiatry should deal with?

   a. The word "communicate" is generally understood to refer to nonverbal as well as verbal behavior within a social context. Thus "communication" can mean "interaction" or "transaction." "Communication" also includes all those symbols and clues used by persons in giving and receiving meaning.

   b. Taken in this sense, the communication techniques which people use can be seen as reliable indicators of interpersonal functioning.

   c. As an aid to therapy, a study of communication can help close the gap between inference and observation as well as help document the relationship between patterns of communication and symptomatic behavior.*

---

*Jackson, Riskin and I demonstrated this several years ago in a paper analyzing five minutes of a taped family conversation which was sent to us without identifying data by Dr. Lyman Wynne (40).

2. People must communicate clearly if they are going to get the information which they need from others. Without communication we, as humans, would not be able to survive.

   a. We need to find out about the world. We learn to differentiate and relate ourselves to objects by learning how to label them and by learning, through words and experience, what we can expect from them.

   b. We need to find out about other people and about the nature of relationships.
      — What, for example, are the socially approved ways to act, ways expected by others?
      — What behavior will please or displease others?
      — Why do others respond as they do? What are they after? What are their intentions toward us? What are they reporting about themselves?
      — How do we appear to others? How do others see us, evaluate us, react to us?

   c. We receive this vital information in two basic ways:
      — We ask for verbal responses.
      — We also observe nonverbal behavior.

3. People must communicate clearly if they are going to be able to *give* information to others. We need to let others know what is going on inside us.

   a. What we have learned or what we think we know.

   b. What we expect of others.

   c. How we interpret what others do.

   d. What behavior pleases us, displeases us.

   e. What our own intentions are.

   f. How others appear to us.

4. Let us examine in this chapter the difficulties posed by simple verbal communication.

a. For one thing, the same word can have different
meanings, different *denotations.*
— For example, if B asks us "What class are you in?" it
is not clear whether he is asking us what we are
taking in school or what social standing we have.
— In the United States, "Let's *table* that motion" means
"Let's put it aside." In England, the same phrase
means "Let's bring it up for discussion."

b. For another thing, the same word can have different
connotations.
— For example, "mother" is a woman who bears and/or
rears a child (denotation). But "mother" can be a
warm, accepting, nurturing woman or a cold,
demanding, unresponsive woman (connotation).
— When B uses the word "mother," what connotation
does the word carry for him?

c. What compounds the problem is that words are
abstractions, symbols which only stand for referents.
— The symbol is not the same as the "thing" or "idea" or
"observation" for which it stands (although we often
behave verbally as if symbols are literally what they
symbolize). Very often the symbol and its meaning are
assumed to be synonymous.
— Also, words are at different levels of abstraction. We
have words about objects, words about relationships
between objects, words about inner states, words about
other words, words about words about words.
— As words become more abstract, their meanings can
become increasingly obscure.
— Finally, there are many aspects of experience which
are not describable by words.

5. This elementary "meaning of words" aspect of
communication is very important because people so often get
into tangles with each other simply because A was using a
word in one way, and B received the word as if it meant
something entirely different.

a. An excellent example of this might be when A says, "I
was only a *little* late," and B says, "You were *not!*"

    b.   Because words themselves are often unclear, it is important for people to clarify and qualify what they say, and to ask others to do the same when they find themselves puzzled or confused.

6. Words are tools which people use to give and get information. If a person fails to realize that words are only abstractions he will tend to overgeneralize, and he will fall into the error of making the following assumptions:*

    a.   He will assume that one instance is an example of all instances. He will be unclear, particularly in his use of who, what, where, and when.
       — He may use the concept *who* as follows:

          "Everybody is like that."

          "Nobody likes me."

          "All women are . . ."

          "Men are . . ."
       — He may use the concept *what* as follows:

          "Nothing turns out right."

          "Everything is all fouled up."
       — He may use the concept *where* as follows:

          "Everywhere I go, that happens."

          "Nowhere is it any different."
       — He may use the concept *when* as follows:

          "Never is it any different."

          "Always this happens to me."

---

*I am indebted here to William Pemberton's article, "Non-Directive Reorientation in Counseling" (52).

b. He will assume that other people share his feelings, thoughts, perceptions:

> "How can you like fish!"

> "Why didn't you do it the *right* way?"

> "Of course he wouldn't want that!"

c. He will assume that his perceptions or evaluations are complete:

> "Yes, I already know about that."

d. He will assume that what he perceives or evaluates won't change:

> "That's the way she is."

> "I've always been that way."

> "That's life."

e. He assumes that there are only two possible alternatives when assessing perceptions or evaluations; he dichotomizes or thinks in terms of black or white:

> "She either loves me or she doesn't."

> "That will either make him or break him."

> "You're either for me or against me."

f. He assumes that characteristics which he attributes to things or people are part of those things or people:

> "That picture is ugly."

> "He is selfish."

> "She is hostile."

g. He assumes that he can get inside the head of another. He operates as if from a "crystal ball" and he acts as a spokesman for others:

"I know what you're thinking."

"I know what she *really* means."

"I will tell you what she was feeling."

"This is what he was going through."

h. He also assumes that the other can get inside his head. He assumes that the other also has a crystal ball. He allows the other to be a spokesman for him:

"She knows what I think."

"You know what I *really* mean."

"He can tell you what I went through."

7. If the receiver of these messages is as dysfunctional a communicator as the sender, he will respond by either agreeing or disagreeing.

a. If he agrees, clear communication will not have taken place, since he cannot be sure what it is to which he is agreeing. He may say:

"That picture *is* ugly, isn't it."

"She *is* selfish, isn't she."

"Yes, she *was* feeling such and such."

"Yes, women *are* like that."

"That certainly *is* the right way."

b. If he disagrees, he still cannot be sure with what he is disagreeing. However, the fact that he does disagree can stimulate either him or the sender to clarify their messages later. He may say:

"That picture is *not* ugly. It is beautiful."

"She is *not* selfish. She is very generous."

"No, she was *not* feeling that. What she was
feeling was . . ."

"No, women aren't like that. They're . . ."

"No, that isn't the right way. *This* is the right way."

8. If the receiver, in this interchange, is a functional
communicator, he will not stop either to agree or disagree.
He will first ask the sender to clarify and qualify. He
may say:

"What do you mean when you say that picture is
ugly?"

"What does she do that strikes you as selfish?"

"How can you tell what I'm thinking? You aren't
me."

"What do you mean, 'everybody' is like that? Do you
mean your wife, your boss, or who?"

"Do you mean *all* women or just the women you
have known?"

"What doesn't turn out right? What in particular?"

"Where, exactly, have such things happened to you?
At home? At work?"

"Why does it surprise you that I like fish? *You*
don't, but that doesn't mean *I* don't."

"What do you mean by doing something the 'right'
way? Do you mean *your* way, or what?"

9. Once the sender receives such requests to clarify and
qualify, how does he respond to them?

a. If he is a functional communicator, he may say:

"Let me try to re-state that another way."

"Maybe I should give some examples."

"I operate from a certain assumption on this, I guess. Here's what I must be assuming . . ."

"I overgeneralized, didn't I? I'll try to pin that down a bit more."

"I'm giving my impression. Maybe you don't share it. How do you see it?"

b. If the original sender is a dysfunctional communicator, he can respond to requests to clarify or qualify in a multitude of different ways. But all these ways tend to shut out feedback from the other.
— He may openly rebuff such requests:

"You know perfectly well what I mean."

"I couldn't be any clearer."

"You heard me."
— He may restate his case without altering it:

"As I said, women are . . ."
— He may re-emphasize his case, without altering it:

"Women are not only X, they are also Y."

"That picture is not only ugly, it is positively revolting."
— He may accuse the questioner:

"Why get so 'picky'?"

"You don't understand plain language."

"Must you 'peel and shred'?"
— He may evade the questions. (See pages 86–88 for an elaboration of this communication technique.)

10. If the original sender responds in a functional way to requests for clarification and qualification, then the receiver of his message has a better idea of what is being discussed. He may then say:

> "Oh, that's what you meant! I misunderstood you."

> "Well, we have different ideas about that. Let's see how we arrived at them."

> "I don't share your experiences, I guess."

> "Yes, I've had similar experiences, but I came to slightly different conclusions. Here's what I decided . . ."

> "Maybe we are hung up on words. Here's what I mean by . . ."

11. If the sender had clarified and qualified his messages in the first place, the interchange would have had less chance of going awry. He might have said:

> "Many people, at least the ones I have known, seem like that."

> "This often happens to me, particularly at work."

> "I find it hard to see how anyone could like fish. Maybe that's because I hate it."

> "This way has worked for me. Maybe it would for you."

> "I wouldn't *expect* him to want that. I wouldn't want it myself."

> "I would call her selfish, but then she is probably different with other people. How is she with you?"

> "To me, women are such and such. Do you agree?"

> "I got the impression, from what you said, that you meant to do such and such. Did I size you up right?"

12. In summary, a person who communicates in a functional way can:

    a. Firmly state his case,

    b. yet at the same time clarify and qualify what he says,

    c. as well as ask for feedback,

    d. and be receptive to feedback when he gets it.

13. If verbal communication is to be reasonably clear, both the sender of a message and the receiver have the responsibility to make it so.

    a. Mutual clarification and qualification cuts down on generalizations.
        — It enables both parties to be specific and to give evidence for their assertions.
        — It enables one person to check out his "reality" against the other person's "reality."

    b. It also helps to separate the perceiver from what is being perceived.
        — It cuts down on the tendency to project one's own wishes, thoughts, perceptions, onto others.
        — It cuts down on the efforts of one person to speak for another.

14. Of course, none of us communicate this ideally or intellectually.

    a. We all generalize when we communicate.

    b. Anyone who perpetually clarified and qualified would seem just as dysfunctional as the person who rarely did so. He might even lead the receiver to wonder if there was anyone in the interaction to interact *with*.

    c. A sender who perpetually asked a receiver for feedback would put himself in the position of being inundated by it and never formulating his own case.

d. A receiver who perpetually asked a sender to clarify would seem testy, uncooperative, and irritating.

15. Generalizations are dangerous, if overused, but they are also indispensable shortcuts.

a. They help us organize our experience.

b. They help us talk about a multitude of different observations all at once.

c. They free us from the necessity of evaluating every new event afresh.

d. Theory itself is a body of generalizations. As such it has been a useful tool in all the sciences.

16. But the person who communicates dysfunctionally behaves as though he is not aware of the fact that he generalizes or that he operates from assumptions.

a. He rarely checks out or specifies how he or others are using words.

b. He overgeneralizes.

c. His communication techniques only serve to becloud meaning, and he seems to have no way to get back on the communication track when he gets off of it.

17. Dysfunctional people also send incomplete messages.

a. They do not complete their sentences, but rely on the receiver to fill in:

"He isn't very . . . *you* know."

"As you can see . . . well, it's obvious."

b. They use pronouns vaguely. (Such communication problems repeatedly show up in family therapy.)

W: We went and so they got upset.

Th: Wait a minute. *Who* went *where? Who* got upset?

W: Oh, well, Harry and I went to his mother's house, see—Harry's mother's house. The kids wanted to go but Harry and I wanted to go alone. So the kids cried as we left the house.

c. They leave out whole connections in their messages.

Th: (to wife) I'm sorry I was late to our appointment today.

W: Oh that's all right. Mark was running around the block.

Filled in, such a message becomes:

Oh that's all right. My dog got out of the house (my dog's name is Mark) and was running around the block. I had to run after him. It took some time to catch him. So I was late to our appointment, too.

d. Often, they do not send a message at all but behave, in relation to others, as if they had. (This comes up repeatedly in therapy, and is usually related to an inside wish which never gets into words.)

M: They never help around the house.

Th: Now you mean the kids?

M: Yes.

Th: Have you told them what you want them to do?

M: Well, I think so. They're supposed to know.

Th: But have you *told* them?

M: Well, no.

* * * * * * *

W: We had no bread for dinner. He forgot.

Th: You mean your husband?

W: Yes.

Th: (to husband) Did you know that you were out of bread in the house?

H: No, heck no, I didn't. . . .

Th: Do you remember her telling you?

H: No. No, she never told me. If I had known, I would have picked some up on the way home.

Th: Do you remember telling him that you were out of bread and asking him to pick some up?

W: Well, maybe I didn't. No, maybe I didn't. But you'd think he'd know.

e. Here is an example which also includes a tangle over the definition of a word:

H: She never comes up to me and kisses me. I am always the one to make the overtures.

Th: Is this the way you see yourself behaving with your husband?

W: Yes, I would say he is the demonstrative one. I didn't know he wanted me to make the overtures.

Th: Have you told your wife that you would like this from her—more open demonstration of affection?

H: Well, no, you'd think she'd know.

W: No, how would I know? You always said you didn't like aggressive women.

H: I don't, I don't like *dominating* women.

W: Well, I thought you meant women who make the overtures. How am I to know what you want?

Th: You'd have a better idea if he had been able to *tell* you.

18. As I said before, absolutely clear communication is impossible to achieve because communication is, by its very nature, incomplete. But there are degrees of incompleteness. The dysfunctional communicator leaves the receiver groping and guessing about what he has inside his head or heart.

   a.   He not only leaves the receiver groping and guessing; he operates from the assumption that he did, in fact, communicate.

   b.   The receiver, in turn, operates from what he guesses.

   c.   It is easy for them to misunderstand one another.

   d.   It is difficult for them to arrive at planned goals or outcomes.

   e.   People need to have a means for completing their communication as much as possible if they are going to arrive at successful joint outcomes, from accomplishing the mundane work of everyday life and seeing that the bread gets on the table, to being able to enjoy mutually satisfying sexual relationships.

19. This is not to say that all incomplete messages are dysfunctional ones. They may be functional and amusing.

   a.   Codes, for instance, are intentionally incomplete messages.
   — They represent shared shortcuts in meaning.
   — People who share a code share something special together.

   b.   But the users of a code must be clear about its meaning. When they get off the communication track through using codes, they must be able to get back on the track by being able to determine when the game is over.

c.   When people have shared experiences, they tend to condense many of them into codes. Therapists do this with patients. "Oh, that's all right, Mark was running around the block," became a code between the family and me, a code which I referred to when family members failed to complete their messages. I also used it to demonstrate that codes *can* be used functionally, if everyone concerned is clear about the meaning. This code got shortened to "Remember Mark" or even just "Mark."

d.   There is a story about codes, which I often tell to patients when they get off the communication track with each other:

> A reporter visited an old men's home and noticed a group of men sitting in the living room. One of the men said "27" and everyone went "ha ha ha." Then another said "15" and everyone went "ha ha ha." Then another said "36" and there was silence.
>
> "What's going on here?" the reporter asked the director, who was showing him around. "You hear all these numbers and then everyone laughs."
>
> "Oh," the director said, "you see, these men have been here for a long time and they know each other's jokes so well that instead of telling them over and over again, they just give the number."
>
> "Well," the reporter asked, "what happened to number '36' then?"
>
> "Oh that fellow!" the director answered, "He never *could* tell a joke."

CHAPTER IX

Communication: A Verbal and Nonverbal Process of Making Requests of the Receiver

1. When judging whether a communication is clear, one must also remember that people communicate in a variety of ways in addition to using words.

   a. A person simultaneously communicates by his gestures, facial expression, body posture and movement, tone of voice, and even by the way he is dressed.

   b. And all this communication occurs within a context. When does it take place? Where? With whom? Under what circumstances? What is the contract between the persons carrying on the interchange?

2. Because of all these factors, communication is a complex business. The receiver must assess all the different ways in which the sender is sending messages, as well as being aware of his own receiving system, that is, his own interpretation system.

   a. When A talks, B assesses the verbal meaning of A's message.

   b. He also listens to the tone of voice in which A speaks.

   c.   He also watches what A does; he notes the "body language" and facial expressions which accompany A's message.

   d.   He also assesses what A is saying within a social context. The context may be how B has seen A respond to him and to others in the past. It may also be B's expectations about what the requirements of the situation are.

   e.   In other words, the receiver (B) is busy assessing both the verbal and the nonverbal content of A's message so that he can come to some judgment about what A meant by his communication.

3. What A meant by his communication can be said to have at least two levels:

   a.   *The denotative level:* the literal content.

   b.   *The metacommunicative level:* a comment on the literal content as well as on the nature of the relationship between the persons involved.

4. Animals other than man can send metacommunications. For example, as Gregory Bateson describes it:

   a.   Cats may go through all their battery of fighting motions yet at the same time withhold their claws.

   b.   By this metacommunication the cat clues other cats as well as people to the fact that he is not "really" fighting; he is playing at fighting (22).

5. Metacommunication is a message *about* a message.

   a.   It conveys the sender's attitude toward the message he just sent: "The message I sent was a friendly one."

   b.   It conveys the sender's attitude toward himself: "I am a friendly person."

   c.   It conveys the sender's attitude, feelings, intentions

toward the receiver: "I see you as someone to be friendly with."

6. Humans are especially versatile at metacommunication.

   a. Humans, like other animals, can send nonverbal metacommunications. But the variety of these is wide; humans can frown, grimace, smile, stiffen, slump. And the context in which humans communicate is, itself, one way of communicating.

   b. As a matter of fact, humans cannot communicate without, at the same time, metacommunicating. Humans cannot *not* metacommunicate.

   c. Humans can also send verbal metacommunications. They can verbally explain their message-sending.

7. When a person verbally explains his message-sending, he is thus denotatively speaking at a metacommunicative level. And these verbal metacommunications are, themselves, at various abstraction levels.

   a. A person can label what kind of message he sent telling the receiver how seriously he wishes him to receive it and how he should respond to it. He can say:

      "It was a joke." (laugh at it)

      "It was just a passing remark" (ignore it)

      "It was a question." (answer it)

      "It was a request." (consider it)

      "It was an order." (obey it)

   b. He can say why he sent the message, by referring to what the other did.

      "You hit me. So I hit you back."

      "You were kind to me. I was returning the favor."

c. He can say why he sent the message, by referring to what he thinks the other's wishes, feelings, intentions toward him are.

> "I thought you were mad and were going to hurt me."

> "I thought you were tired and wanted me to help you."

> "I thought you were discouraged and wanted me to reassure you."

d. He can say why he sent the message by referring to a request made by the other:

> "You were ordering me to do something, and I don't take orders."

> "You were requesting something from me, and I was considering it."

e. He can say why he sent the message by referring to the kind of response which he was trying to elicit from the other:

> "I was trying to get your goat."

> "I was trying to get you to love me."

> "I was trying to get you to talk."

> "I was trying to make you laugh."

> "I was trying to get you to agree with me."

f. He can say why he sent the message by specifically referring to what he was trying to get the other to do or say or *not* do and *not* say:

> "I wanted you to go to the store for me."

> "I was asking you to phone her for me."

> "I was asking you to leave the room."

"I didn't want you to tell her about my illness."

"I wanted you to tell him that I was home."

8. Since humans can "metacommunicate" both verbally and nonverbally, they can give the receiver quite an assortment of messages to sort and weigh, as he tries to figure out what is meant by the communication.

   a. Perhaps A makes the following denotative statement: "The dog is on the couch."

   b. He automatically comments, nonverbally, on this statement, by the irritable tone in which he makes it.

   c. He can then verbally explain what he meant by what he said. Out of the welter of choices, he may say: "I wanted you to take the dog off the couch."

9. The receiver of these messages (B) must balance what A said, with how he said it, with what he then said about it.

   a. B balances the nonverbal and the verbal metacommunications (within the context) and compares them to the denotative statement.

   b. If they are all congruent (seem to jibe with each other) he has little difficulty in deciding that A meant what he said he meant.

   c. Whether or not they jibe, he will attend more to the nonverbal metacommunications and to context than he will to the verbal metacommunications. For one thing, the nonverbal is a less clear or explicit communication, so it requires greater attention.

10. Whenever a person communicates he is not only making a statement, he is also asking something of the receiver and trying to influence the receiver to give him what he wants. This is the "command aspect" of a message. Such requests, however, may have various degrees of explicitness and intensity.

    a.   The sender may be simply asking the receiver to show, by response, that his message was heard: "Just listen to me."

    b.   Or he may be asking for a specific kind of response: "Tell me where the store is" or, "Go to the store for me."

11. The receiver, in turn, must respond, because people cannot *not* communicate.

    a.   Even if the receiver remains silent, he is still communicating.

    b.   And, incidentally, symptoms are one way of communicating in a nonverbal way.

12. But even though all messages have requests in them, they are not always expressed verbally. Thus, the receiver must rely on metacommunications for his clues as to what the sender wants. He asks himself:

    a.   What is the sender verbally saying?

    b.   What, specifically, is he requesting? Is the request fully expressed at the denotative level?

    c.   If not, perhaps the way in which he communicates and the context in which he is communicating will give me clues to what he is asking of me.

13. If the communication, or message, and the metacommunication or meta-message do not fit, the receiver must somehow translate this into a single message. In order to do this satisfactorily he needs to be able to comment on the presence of the discrepancy. Let us take a trivial example. A husband who is working on a household fixture says, in an irritable tone, "Damn it, the fixture broke!" The

wife, in this relationship, may go through the following process (with greater agility and speed, of course, than the snail's pace described here):

a. He is telling me about the condition of the electrical fixture he is working on.

b. But he is doing more than that. He is telling me that he is irritated. His "Damn it," along with his tone, helps me decide this.

c. Is he criticizing me? Is he telling me that I am responsible for the condition of the fixture?

d. If he is criticizing me, what does he want me to do? Take over the job for him? Apologize? Or what?

e. Or is he criticizing himself, irritated that he is having a frustrating time with the job, and that he only has himself to blame for the fact that the fixture broke?

f. If he is primarily criticizing himself, what is he asking me to do? Sympathize with him? Listen to him? Or what?

g. I know, from living with him, that he prides himself on his tool dexterity and that he considers electrical maintenance his special forte. Evidently, his view of himself is being put to the test. So he must be criticizing himself. And he must primarily be asking me to sympathize with him.

h. But sympathize *how*? Does he want me to help him with the job, bring him coffee, or what? What behavior on my part that he could see and hear would mean to him that I am sympathizing with him?

14. Let us take another example. A husband says, in an irritable tone, "The dog is on the couch." The wife, in this relationship, may go through the following process:

a. He is telling me where the dog is.

b. But he is doing more than that. He sounds irritated.

c. Why is he telling me about his irritation? Is he criticizing me for the fact that the dog is on the couch?

d. If he is not criticizing me, what does he want me to do? Just listen to him? Sympathize with his irritation? Take the dog off the couch? Or what?

e. I wanted a dog. He didn't. I went ahead and got one without his agreement. Now, when he shows his irritation at the dog, he is complaining about what I did. He is criticizing me for disobeying him. He undoubtedly wants me to take the dog off the couch, but does he also want me to get rid of the dog and apologize to him for going against his wishes?

15. Let us return to the first example. Instead of saying, "Damn it, the fixture broke", the husband could say, "Damn it, I'm having a hard time with this job. Bring me a cup of coffee." The wife, in this case, would have little trouble assessing his message. He would be telling her overtly what he wanted from her and why. In other words, his request that she sympathize with him by bringing coffee would be clear.

16. In the second example, instead of saying, "The dog is on the couch," the husband could say, "Take the dog off the couch and get rid of him. You never should have bought a dog. I told you I didn't want one." The wife in this case would have little trouble assessing his message.

a. He would be telling her specifically what he wanted from her and why. In other words, his request that she agree to obey him would be clear.

b. In both cases, the wife is still in the position of deciding whether or not to agree to her husband's request that she obey him. But at least she is in no doubt about what it really is that her husband wants of her.

17. In other words, the request, which is part of every message, may or may not be expressed denotatively. And there are degrees to which requests can be spelled out denotatively.

a. "Damn it, the fixture broke," and "The dog is on the couch," are very indirect requests, requests not expressed at the denotative level.

b. "Bring me a cup of coffee," and "Take the dog off the couch and get rid of him," are direct requests, requests expressed at the denotative level.

c. Or, if these specific requests had been expressed at a more abstract level, they would also be direct: "Sympathize with me" or "Do what I want."

18. However, all messages, when viewed at their highest abstraction level can be characterized as "Validate me" messages. These are frequently interpreted as "Agree with me," "Be on my side," "Validate me by sympathizing with me," or, "Validate me by showing me you value me and my ideas."

19. When people communicate, they rarely go around verbally requesting that others agree with them or requesting that others want what they want. They don't, because they are forced by the wish to be valued, and by the wish for cooperation, to persuade or at least try to elicit the wished-for response. Many persons feel embarrassed about their wish to get validation from outside themselves.

a. As I have said, communication is a necessarily incomplete process. But we can now see why this process becomes even more incomplete than pure logic or inadequacy of words would dictate.

b. Incomplete (indirect) communication can serve many interpersonal purposes which are not necessarily dysfunctional.
— It can help camouflage such requests.
— It can prevent embarrassment in case one's requests (of any kind) are refused.

20. Up to now, I have been discussing the problems posed for human receivers by the complexity and the incompleteness of human communication.

a. Just because this communication *is* complex and incomplete to differing degrees, all receivers are required to fill in or complete the sender's message by clairvoyance or guesswork.

b. Receivers can and do achieve this, sometimes with amazing accuracy, considering all the fancy footwork they have to go through.

c. But there are times when even the most clairvoyant of receivers guesses incorrectly. When this happens, the sender's next message usually lets him know his error.

21. The messages I have listed in this chapter have all been relatively *congruent* within the context; they have jibed with each other.

a. A congruent communication is one where two or more messages are sent via different levels but none of these messages seriously contradicts any other. For example, the husband says, "The dog is on the couch," in an irritable tone, in a context which tells the wife that he is irritated and why he is irritated.

b. An incongruent communication is one where two or more messages, sent via different levels, seriously do contradict each other. One level of communication is context itself. For example, the husband says, in a delighted tone, that the dog is on the couch, but from the context the wife knows that he hates dogs; whether they are on couches or anywhere else.

22. Simple contradictory communication is where two or more messages are sent in a sequence via the same communication level and oppose each other.

a. Perhaps A says the following:

"Come here . . . No, go away."

"I love you . . . No, I hate you."

"I'm happy . . . No, I'm sad."

"My wife is tall . . . No, my wife is short."

   b.   Perhaps A does the following:
       — Pushes B away. Pulls B back.
       — Buys a ticket to the movie, but doesn't go see it.
       — Puts his coat on, then takes it off.

23. But such simple contradictions cannot occur without some accompanying metacommunication, since one cannot *not* metacommunicate.

   a.   Although the self-contradictions listed above are relatively clear, they are also accompanied by smiles or frowns or tone of voice, and in a context.

   b.   When contradictions occur between different levels of communication, they become *incongruent.* *

24. Messages differ in the degree to which they are incongruent. Relatively simple incongruent communication sounds and looks like this:

   a.   A says, "It's cold in here," and takes off his coat.

   b.   A says, "I hate you," and smiles.

   c.   A wears an evening dress to a funeral.

   d.   A wears tennis shoes to a board of directors' meeting.

   e.   A says, "Come closer, darling," and then stiffens.

25. Incongruent communication can become even more so when the sender's nonverbal metacommunication does not jibe with his verbal metacommunication.

   a.   The sender may say "Come closer, darling," then stiffen, and then say, "I want to make love."

---

*"Incongruent" refers to a discrepancy between the report and the command aspects of a message; for the system for analyzing this devised by Bateson, Jackson, Haley and Weakland, see 23, 32, 37, and 40 in the bibliography.

— In this case, should the receiver respond to the sender's denotative statement ("Come closer, darling.")?

— Or should he respond to the sender's nonverbal statement (the stiffness)?

— Or should he respond to the sender's words explaining his intentions ("I want to make love.")?

— This is called being presented with a double-level message.

b. As usual, the receiver relies heavily on context, and on the nonverbal signals to help him in his clairvoyance process. In this case, the nonverbal signals and the context contradict each other. But, being an especially trusting and courageous receiver, he says to himself:

> "Let's see. The sender and I are courting. Yet other people are around.
>
> "I have learned from past experience with the sender that she is nervous about showing amorous feelings publicly. But that doesn't mean she doesn't have amorous feelings toward me.
>
> "I will live dangerously and ignore her nonverbal metacommunication in this case. I will rely on context alone and accept her verbally-stated intention.
>
> "In other words, her verbal statement 'I want to make love' carries greater weight with me. All I do is add to it the proviso which she did not add: '. . . but other people are around, so I am just nervous.' In other words, the sender is willing to be nervous, with a little assistance."

c. The freedom to comment and question immediately takes the receiver out of the clairvoyant dilemma. When this freedom is not present, the chances for misunderstanding are great. In the case of a child, as we have seen, there is a likelihood that such messages will be built up to the point where a "double bind" occurs (see page 36).

26. Incongruent communication like that just described puts an extra burden on the receiver. But, whether or not the sender's message is incongruent, the receiver can still go through various checking-out procedures in order to find out what is being reported, what requested, and why.

   a. For example, when the wife heard her husband say, in an irritable tone, "Damn it, the fixture broke," she could have decided that she still didn't have enough data, even from the content of the message, to find out what her husband was requesting from her and why.

   b. She might have gone to where he was and stood there for a minute, continuing to pick up clues from him.
      — If she had done this, she would, of course, have been communicating with him. By her presence she would be saying: "I heard you. I am attending."
      — He would also continue to communicate with her, as he jabbed at the fixture, grunted, sighed, etc.

   c. The wife might then have asked, "Is there anything I can do?"
      — The minute she did this, she would be asking her husband to be specific in what he was requesting.
      — Perhaps he would have said, "No, I just have to work it out."
      — By this response, the wife would have succeeded in narrowing her unknowns. She would now be more certain that he was distressed with himself but she still could not be sure what he specifically wanted from her. Did he want her to listen? Attend? Sympathize?

   d. The wife might go on to ask, "Would you like a cup of coffee?" And he might answer, "Yes, damn it, I would." The communication sequence would now be relatively closed or complete. (Of course, it is more complete if she actually brings the coffee!)

27. If, instead, the wife had been fairly confident about her clairvoyance, she might have simply assumed that she knew what his implied request was. She might have put it in words herself and seen how he responded.

a. She could have asked outright, "Would you like a cup of coffee?" and he might have said, "Yes, damn it, I would." If she had guessed correctly enough, the sequence would have been relatively closed.

b. But he might have said, "Hell, no, what would I want coffee for, at a time like this?" Then she would have known that her clairvoyance process wasn't working very well. She would have been required to check out further, perhaps by going through the clue-getting procedures already described.

28. Receivers vary in their ability to perceive the needs and wishes of others.

a. Although all receivers put great weight on the metacommunicative aspects, they vary in their ability to assess what the sender is asking of them.
— The wife may mistake her husband's irritation with himself for a criticism of her, and end up trying to take over the job for him instead of sympathizing with him.
— The wife may mistake her husband's criticism of her for irritation over the specific behavior of the dog, and end up trying to sympathize with him instead of taking the dog off the couch or getting rid of the dog.
— The lover, in the third example, may mistake the woman's stiffening for distaste, and end up rejecting her instead of making love.

b. We even have psychiatric labels for people who are not able to accurately weigh a message for its meaning. They are not able to guess attitudes, intentions, feelings (as expressed in metacommunication) accurately.

c. If this wife, in all contexts, in all relationships, and at all times within a relationship, decides that senders are criticizing her or praising her, we would readily label her paranoid or egocentric.

d. Also, although receivers put great weight on the metacommunicative aspects to help tell them what the sender is requesting, they vary in their ability to attend to denotation in spite of, or along with, metacommunication. For example, perhaps a person attends a lecture for the purpose of receiving denotative content from the speaker. But perhaps the speaker speaks in such a frightened tone that the receiver cannot hear what the speaker is saying because he is so concerned about the speaker's fright.

29. Senders vary in their ability to send clear requests, so that the receiver has to guess as little as possible.

    a.   For example, let us say that a wife wants to see a movie with her husband. If she communicates in a functional way, she might say, "Let's see a movie," or, more overtly, "I would like to see a movie with you."

    b.   But, if she communicates in a dysfunctional way, she might say any of the following things:

> "You would like to see a movie, *wouldn't* you."

> "It would do you good to see a movie."

> "If you want to see a movie, we'll see one."

> "We might as well see a movie. It's Saturday night."

> "There's a new movie house down the street."

> "My voices are ordering me to see a movie."

30. These are some of the covert ways in which this wife can request something from her husband without acknowledging that she is making a request.

    a.   She does not clearly label her wish which is behind her request, as *her* wish.

    b.   Or, she may fail to label her wish *as a wish*. It becomes not a wish but a "must," something one is commanded to do. (The commander may be the other person or people in general, or "one's duty" or "voices" or something foreign inside of the self.)

c. Or, she may label her wish as not a wish but as "the lesser of two evils."

31. The husband, in this case, could do some checking out. He could say: "Do *you* want to see a movie?" or "Do you want to see a movie *with me?*"

   a. But here is what can happen if the husband does ask his wife what she meant by her communication. She might go on to explain her message in any one of the following statements:

   "No, I thought *you* wanted to go."

   "No, I just thought we *should.*"

   "No, I don't necessarily want to go. I want to do what you want."

   "There are times when I want to see a movie, but this isn't one of them."

   "I don't particularly want to go. My voices are ordering me."

32. By denying that she had a wish, the wife is also denying that her wish was expressed toward her husband. She denies that she has made a request of him. If he pursues his questions, she may go on to deny further.

   "You can go or not. I don't care."

   "If you want to be a stay-at-home, that's your business."

   "If you go to the movies, you go to the movies."

   "Nobody asked you to go. If you want to go, then go."

33. The wife, when replying to her husband's request (in this case, a request to clarify), denies any or all parts of her message.

a. The Bateson group, and Jay Haley, in particular, has defined four parts of every message:
— I (the sender)
— am saying something (message)
— to you (the receiver)
— in this situation (context) (33).

b. All messages are requests, yet the wife may deny this, in so many words, by saying:

> "I didn't care one way or the other." (*I* didn't request anything.)

> "I just threw out a suggestion for whatever it was worth." (I didn't *request* anything.)

> "Whether or not you go to the movies is immaterial to me." (I didn't request anything *of you.*)

> "At one time, I might have wanted to go with you. But I know better now." (I didn't request anything of you *just now.*)

34. We note how defensive the wife is, as she sends her highly incomplete message. (These messages are incomplete because they do not clearly label *"I, want this, from you, in this situation."*) She makes it hard for her husband to find out what she wants.

a. She covers herself as she sends her request, almost as though she anticipated refusal.

> "Voices are ordering me . . ."

> "I am doing this for you . . ."

> "There's a new movie house down the street."

b. She covers herself after she is asked to clarify: "I thought*you* wantedmetogo,"or,"Nobodyaskedyoutogo."

35. We also note how offensive the wife is, as she sends her request and responds to requests to clarify. She makes it hard for her husband to want to do what she wants.

a. She disparages him in anticipation of refusal:

> "A person should see a movie at least once a month if he professes to be cultured."

> "We might as well see a movie. I'm bored."

b. She disparages him after he asks her to clarify (and this very disparagement reveals her disappointment over the fact that he does not seem influenceable):

> "I can't *make* you do anything."

> "You'll do exactly what you *feel* like doing."

> "Ask anything of you? I know better!"

36. One could decide, on first thought, that this wife is a dysfunctional communicator and that she puts unnecessary burdens on her functional husband who, in this case, tries to check out the meaning of her message.

a. But when people communicate, they are sending a message to a receiver.

b. The wife tailors her message to the way she thinks her husband will respond to it.

c. Once we note how he does respond to her, we will see that her messages are tailored to a kind of response which she has learned to expect from her husband.

d. Her husband, in his response, does the same.

37. One cannot view messages separate from interaction, as I have been doing, and receive the full picture.

a. One must at least note what A says, how B responds, how A responds to B's response. Communication is a two-sided affair; senders are receivers, receivers are also senders.

b. One must note whether or not these interaction sequences repeat themselves over time and in different content areas.

c. If they do repeat themselves, these sequences represent how these two people characteristically communicate with one another.

38. However, before analyzing interaction, one can profit from analyzing isolated messages. Such an analysis:

a. Highlights different principles about messages and message-sending.

b. Highlights the kinds of problems which highly defensive communication poses for the receiver.

c. Helps document inferences about what inner wishes and fears dictate and how they perpetuate dysfunctional communication.

39. This husband's communication does have something to do with the wife's characteristic way of asking for something from him.

a. But even before analyzing this, we can guess that this wife fears that her husband will reject her request.

b. Behind her denials that she has a wish and has made a request, is the wish that her husband would not only want to go to the movies with her, but would want to do what she wants because he loves her: "You'll do what you *feel* like doing".

c. She is not unusual in having this want. But if she cannot come to terms with it, she can easily trap herself and her husband in an impossible dilemma.
— No two people think alike on everything.
— No two people feel the same way at all times within a relationship.
— No two people want the same things or want them at the same time. People operate from different timetables.

— We are, in fact, autonomous, different, and unique
   beings.
— Yet we are, at the same time, dependent on others.
   We need them to help us get many of the things we
   want (or not prevent us from getting them). We are
   also dependent on others to validate our existence
   and worth.

40. Therefore, even though people are making requests of others
    when they communicate, there are some things that cannot
    be requested. Yet these are the very things people also want.

   a. We cannot ask that others feel as we do or as we want
      them to. As Bateson and Watzlawick have pointed out,
      feelings are spontaneous; they are not subject to
      self-request or to the requests of others (22, 138).
      — All we can do is try to elicit feelings.
      — Failing to elicit, we can accept our disappointment
         and try again.

   b. We cannot ask that others think as we do. Thoughts are
      not subject to the requests of others.
      — All we can do is try to persuade others, and present
         our arguments in the clearest, most cogent form
         possible.
      — Failing to persuade, we can accept our
         disappointment and compromise, or "agree to
         disagree."

   c. We can, of course, *demand* that others say or do (or not
      say or not do) what we want. But if we succeed in this,
      our success will be questionable.
      — We shall have validated our power but not our
         lovability or worth, since we have "had to ask."
      — Also, since such a tactic challenges the other's
         autonomy, it is likely that he will feel devalued and
         will devalue back.

41. Evidently man is insatiable. He can never be loved enough,
    valued enough. Yet he can never be safe enough, powerful
    enough.

a. These two wants are contradictory if viewed on the same continuum. Man seems to have a built-in potential for defeating himself.
   — If he sees these two wants as an either/or proposition, he puts them in conflict with each other and loses out on both.
   — If he allows them to coexist, each in its proper time and place, he will not only gain both, but will find that each enhances the other.

b. The way he communicates with other persons will take its form from whichever of these two approaches he adopts.
   — If he takes the first approach, it indicates that he will handle the different-ness of others in terms of *war* and *who is right*.
   — If he takes the second, he will handle different-ness on the basis of *exploration* and *what fits*.
   — The former leads to stalemating, retardation and pathology.
   — The latter leads to growth, individuality and creativity.

c. In the next chapter, I shall be going into this question of how dysfunctional and functional communication express and influence pathology and health.

PART THREE: THEORY AND PRACTICE OF THERAPY

CHAPTER X

Concepts of Therapy

---

1. In this chapter, I should like to restate in a more general
   way some of the ideas about psychic health and illness
   which we have discussed previously, in order to show their
   relevance to the interactional approach of family therapy. I
   also want to present my own picture of what a family
   therapist is and does, since he becomes, to an important
   degree, a model for his patients' subsequent behavior.

   I am not trying to present a "philosophy of therapy." These
   ideas appear to me as working tools, helpful in organizing
   my own way of handling therapy, or as a conceptual core
   around which therapeutic growths may be structured, rather
   than as a system of thought possessing value in and for
   itself.

   Finally, let me say that this discussion of theory is
   admittedly schematic, not filled in. I intend to follow this
   volume with a later one in which I will be illustrating my
   basis of operations more fully with examples from actual
   family situations.

2. The most important concept in therapy, because it is a
   touchstone for all the rest, is that of *maturation*.

117

    a.   This is the state in which a given human being is fully in charge of himself.

    b.   A mature person is one who, having attained his majority, is able to make choices and decisions based on accurate perceptions about himself, others, and the context in which he finds himself; who acknowledges these choices and decisions as being his; and who accepts responsibility for their outcomes.

3. The patterns of behaving that characterize a mature person we call functional because they enable him to deal in a relatively competent and precise way with the world in which he lives. Such a person will:

    a.   manifest himself clearly to others.

    b.   be in touch with signals from his internal self, thus letting himself know openly what he thinks and feels.

    c.   be able to see and hear what is outside himself as differentiated from himself and as different from anything else.

    d.   behave toward another person as someone separate from himself and unique.

    e.   treat the presence of different-ness as an opportunity to learn and explore rather than as a threat or a signal for conflict.

    f.   deal with persons and situations in their context, in terms of "how it is" rather than how he wishes it were or expects it to be.

    g.   accept responsibility for what he feels, thinks, hears and sees, rather than denying it or attributing it to others.

    h.   have techniques for openly negotiating the giving, receiving and checking of meaning between himself and others.*

---

*This description of maturity emphasizes social and communication skills rather than the acquisition of knowledge and recognized achievement, which in my view derive from the first two.

4. We call an individual dysfunctional when he has not learned to communicate properly. Since he does not manifest a means of perceiving and interpreting himself accurately, or interpreting accurately messages from the outside, the assumptions on which he bases his actions will be faulty and his efforts to adapt to reality will be confused and inappropriate.

   a. As we have seen, the individual's communication problems are rooted in the complex area of family behavior in which he lived as a child. The adults in the family provide the blueprint by which the child grows from infancy to maturity.

   b. If the male and female who were his survival figures did not manage jointly, if their messages to each other and the child were unclear and contradictory, he himself will learn to communicate in an unclear and contradictory way.

5. A dysfunctional person will manifest himself incongruently, that is, he will deliver conflicting messages, via different levels of communication and using different signals.

   a. As an example, let us take the behavior of the parents of a disturbed child during their first interview with the therapist. When the therapist asks what seems to be the trouble, they practically deny that there is any.

      M: Well, I don't know. I think financial problems more than anything . . . outside of that, we're a very close family.

      F: We do everything together. I mean, we hate to leave the kids. When we go someplace, we take the kids with us. As far as doing things together as a family, we always try to do that at least once a week, say on Sundays, Sunday afternoon, why we always try to get the kids together and take them out for a ride to the park or something like that.

   b. In words, they imply that there is no reason why they should be in a therapist's office. But their actual presence there, and the agreement they have already made to enter therapy, amount to an admission of the contrary. And the father presents a further contradiction when he reduces his claim that the family does "everything" together to a statement about the rides they take on Sunday afternoons.

6. In addition, a dysfunctional individual will be unable to adapt his interpretations to the present context.

  a. He will tend to see the "here and now" through labels which have been indelibly fixed in his mind during the early part of his life when all messages had survival significance. Each subsequent use of the label will strengthen its reality.

  b. Therefore, it is conceivable that he will impose on the present that which fits the past, or that which he expects from the future, thus negating the opportunity to gain a perspective on the past or realistically shape the future.
  — For example, a school-age girl was brought into therapy because she was acting strangely and talking in riddles. When the mother was asked, "When did you notice that your child was not developing as she should?" she replied, "Well, she was a seven-month baby, and she was in an incubator for six weeks." The child's present and past difficulties were thus connected in a very illogical fashion.*
  — Later she said that after she brought the baby home from the hospital, "She wouldn't give me any reaction, just as though she couldn't hear. And I'd take her around and hold her next to me, and she wouldn't pay any attention, and I know it upset me, and I asked the doctor and he said it was nothing, she was just being stubborn—that's one thing that sort of stuck in my mind with her."

---

*The communication aspects of this situation Jackson has labeled "past-present switches." Thus, the answer to the therapist's question, "How out of all the millions of people in the world did you two find each other?" may be as useful in family diagnosis as psychological testing. This question allows the spouses to describe their present relationship under cover of talking about the past. For further examples of this phenomenon, see Watzlawick's *An Anthology of Human Communication* (138).

— By using the word "stubborn" for the baby's
indifference, the mother has given the baby a label
that does not suit the context of babyhood. It implies
that the child can be held accountable for willfully
refusing to return the mother's love. Later on, the
mother applies the same explanation to the child's
strange behavior.

— By using the label "stubborn," and by implying in her
first statement that the child's difficulties have a
physical cause, the mother is able to absolve herself of
blame; in fact, she has a double coverage. It is hard
for such a mother to see her child's present problems
objectively because she has already imposed her own
interpretation on them.

7. Finally, a dysfunctional individual will not be able to
perform the most important function of good
communication: "checking out" his perceptions to see
whether they tally with the situation as it really is or with
the intended meaning of another. When neither of two
people are able to check out their meanings with each other,
the result may resemble a comedy of errors—with a tragic
ending. Here is one possible misunderstanding between a
husband and a wife:

Report: W: "He always yells." H: "I don't yell."

Explanation: W: "I don't do things to suit him." H:
"I don't do things to suit her."

Interpretation: W: "He doesn't care about me." H:
"She doesn't care about me."

Conclusion: W: "I will leave him." H: "I will leave
her."

Manifestation: Wife uses invectives, voice is loud
and shrill, eyes blaze, muscles stand out on base of
neck, mouth is open, nostrils are distended, uses
excessive movements. Husband says nothing, keeps
eyes lowered, mouth tight, body constricted.

Outcome: Wife visits divorce lawyer. Husband files
a counter-suit.

8. Difficulty in communicating is closely linked to an individual's self-concept, that is, his self-image and self-esteem.

    a. His parents may not only have given him inadequate models for *methods* of communication, but the *content* of their messages to him may have been devaluating (see Chapter VI).

    b. In order to form his self-image, the child has a demanding task. He must integrate messages from both parents (separately and together) telling him what to do with aspects of living like dependency, authority, sexuality and coding or labeling (cognition).

    c. If the parents' own attitudes are uncertain, or if they disagree with each other, the messages the child takes will be equally confused. The child will try to integrate what cannot be integrated, on the basis of inconsistent and insufficient data. Failing, he will end up with an incomplete picture of himself and low self-esteem.

    d. In addition, the child's parents may depreciate his self-esteem more directly. He looks to them to validate his steps in growth; if these are not acknowledged at the time they occur, or if they are acknowledged with concomitant messages of disgust, disapproval, embarrassment, indifference or pain, the child's self-esteem will naturally suffer.

9. Low self-esteem leads to dysfunctional communication:

    a. When there is a conflict of interests. Any relationship presupposes a commitment to a joint outcome, an agreement that each partner will give up a little of his own interests in order to reach a wider benefit for both.
      — This outcome is the best objective reality that can be arrived at in terms of what is possible, what is feasible, what fits the best all the way around.
      — The process used for reaching this outcome depends on the self-concepts of the persons engaged in it. If

their self-esteem is low, so that any sacrifice of self seems intolerable, it is likely that the process will be based on some form of deciding "who is right," "who will win," "who is most loved," "who will get mad." I call this the "war syndrome."
— If a person operates by means of this war syndrome, it is inevitable that his ability to seek objective information and arrive at objective conclusions as to what fits will be greatly impaired.

b. Dysfunction in communication will also follow when the individual is unable to handle different-ness.
— As we have seen in Chapter III, an individual who has not achieved an independent selfhood will often take any evidence of different-ness in someone he is close to as an insult or a sign of being unloved.
— This is because he is intensely dependent on the other person to increase his feelings of worth and to validate his self-image. Any reminder that the other is, after all, a separate being, capable of faithlessness and desertion, fills him with fear and distrust.
— Some couples express their objections to each other's different-ness freely and loudly (see the "teeter-totter syndrome," page 17), but others, less secure in this area, prefer to pretend that different-ness does not exist.
— With such couples, communication becomes *covert* (see page 15). Any message which might call attention to the self as a private agent, with likes and dislikes, desires and displeasures of its own, is suppressed or changed. Wishes and decisions are presented as if they emanated from anywhere but inside the speaker himself; statements are disguised as symbolic utterances; messages are left incomplete or even not expressed at all, with the sender relying on mental telepathy to get them across (see pages 84–86). For example, a couple who overtly behaved as if they had absolutely no problems responded in therapy to the "How did you meet?" question as follows:

H: "Well, we were raised in the same neighborhood."

W: "Not exactly the same neighborhood" (laughs).

This slight modification on the wife's part presaged many revelations of serious division between them.

10. Thus far we have been talking about dysfunctional behavior rather than the symptom that calls attention to it. What is the connection between them?

    a. Dysfunctional behavior is, as we have seen, related to feelings of low self-esteem. It is, in fact, a defense against the perception of them. Defenses, in turn, are ways which enable the person with low self-esteem to function *without* a symptom. To the person himself and to the outward world, there may appear to be nothing wrong.

    b. But if he is threatened by some event of survival significance, some happening which says to him, "You do not count; you are not lovable; you are nothing," the defense may prove unequal to the task of shielding him, and a symptom will take its place.

    c. Usually it is only then that the individual and his community will notice that he is "ill" and that he will admit a need for help.

11. How, then, do we define therapy?

    a. If illness is seen to derive from inadequate methods of communication (by which we mean all interactional behavior), it follows that therapy will be seen as an attempt to improve these methods. As will be seen in the chapters on therapy, the emphasis will be on correcting discrepancies in communication and teaching ways to achieve more fitting joint outcomes.

    b. This approach to therapy depends on three primary beliefs about human nature:
      — First, that every individual is geared to survival, growth, and getting close to others and that all behavior expresses these aims, no matter how distorted it may look. Even an extremely disturbed person will be fundamentally on the side of the therapist.

— Second, that what society calls sick, crazy, stupid, or bad behavior is really an attempt on the part of the afflicted person to signal the presence of trouble and call for help. In that sense, it may not be so sick, crazy, stupid, or bad after all.

— Third, that human beings are limited only by the extent of their knowledge, their ways of understanding themselves and their ability to "check out" with others. Thought and feeling are inextricably bound together; the individual need not be a prisoner of his feelings but can use the cognitive component of his feeling to free himself. This is the basis for assuming that a human being can learn what he doesn't know and can change ways of commenting and understanding that don't fit.

12. This brings us to a discussion of the role of the therapist. How will he act? What picture will he have of himself?

   a. Perhaps the best way that he can see himself is as a *resource person.* He is not omnipotent. He is not God, parent or judge. The knotty question for all therapists is how to be an expert without appearing to the patient to be all-powerful, omniscient, or presuming to know always what is right and wrong.

   b. The therapist does have a special advantage in being able to study the patient's family situation as an experienced observer, while remaining outside it, above the power struggle, so to speak. Like a camera with a wide-angle lens, he can see things from the position of each person present and act as a representative of each. He sees transactions, as well as the individuals involved, and thus has a unique viewpoint.

   c. Because of this, the family can place their trust in him as an "official observer," one who can report impartially on what he sees and hears. Above all, he can report on what the family cannot see and cannot report on.

13. The therapist must also see himself as a *model of communication.*

a. First of all, he must take care to be aware of his own prejudices and unconscious assumptions so as not to fall into the trap he warns others about, that of suiting reality to himself. His lack of fear in revealing himself may be the first experience the family has had with clear communication.

b. In addition, the way he interprets and structures the action of therapy from the start is the first step in introducing the family to new techniques in communication.

c. Here is an example of how the therapist clarifies the process of interaction for a family:

Th: (to husband) I notice your brow is wrinkled, Ralph. Does that mean you are angry at this moment?

H: I did not know that my brow was wrinkled.

Th: Sometimes a person looks or sounds in a way of which he is not aware. As far as you can tell, what were you thinking and feeling just now?

H: I was thinking over what she (his wife) said.

Th: What thing that she said were you thinking about?

H: When she said that when she was talking so loud, she wished I would tell her.

Th: What were you thinking about that?

H: I never thought about telling her. I thought she would get mad.

Th: Ah, then maybe that wrinkle meant you were puzzled because your wife was hoping you would do something and you did not know she had this hope. Do you suppose that by your wrinkled brow you were signalling that you were puzzled?

H: Yeh, I guess so.

Th: As far as you know, have you ever been in that same spot before, that is, where you were puzzled by something Alice said or did?

H: Hell, yes, lots of times.

Th: Have you ever told Alice you were puzzled when you were?

W: He never says anything.

Th: (smiling, to Alice) Just a minute, Alice, let me hear what Ralph's idea is of what he does. Ralph, how do you think you have let Alice know when you are puzzled?

H: I think she knows.

Th: Well, let's see. Suppose you ask Alice if she knows.

H: This is silly.

Th: (smiling) I suppose it might seem so in this situation, because Alice is right here and certainly has heard what your question is. She knows what it is. I have the suspicion, though, that neither you nor Alice are very sure about what the other expects, and I think you have not developed ways to find out. Alice, let's go back to when I commented on Ralph's wrinkled brow. Did you happen to notice it, too?

W: (complaining) Yes, he always looks like that.

Th: What kind of a message did you get from that wrinkled brow?

W: He don't want to be here. He don't care. He never talks. Just looks at television or he isn't home.

Th: I'm curious. Do you mean that when Ralph has a wrinkled brow that you take this as Ralph's way of saying, "I don't love you, Alice. I don't care about you, Alice."?

W: (exasperated and tearfully) I don't know.

Th: Well, maybe the two of you have not yet worked out crystal-clear ways of giving your love and value messages to each other. Everyone needs crystal-clear ways of giving their value messages. (to son) What do you know, Jim, about how you give your value messages to your parents?

S: I don't know what you mean.

Th: Well, how do you let your mother, for instance, know that you like her, when you are feeling that way. Everyone feels different ways at different times. When you are feeling glad your mother is around, how do you let her know?

S: I do what she tells me to do. Work and stuff.

Th: I see, so when you do your work at home, you mean this for a message to your mother that you're glad she is around.

S: Not exactly.

Th: You mean you are giving a different message then. Well, Alice, did you take this message from Jim to be a love message? (to Jim) What do you do to give your father a message that you like him?

S: (after a pause) I can't think of nothin'.

Th: Let me put it another way. What do you know crystal-clear that you could do that would bring a smile to your father's face?

S: I could get better grades in school.

Th: Let's check this out and see if you are perceiving clearly. Do you, Alice, get a love message from Jim when he works around the house?

W: I s'pose—he doesn't do very much.

Th: So from where you sit, Alice, you don't get many love messages from Jim. Tell me, Alice, does Jim have any other ways that he might not now be thinking about that he has that say to you that he is glad you are around?

W: (softly) The other day he told me I looked nice.

Th: What about you, Ralph, does Jim perceive correctly that if he got better grades you would smile?

H: I don't imagine I will be smiling for some time.

Th: I hear that you don't think he is getting good grades, but would you smile if he did?

H: Sure, hell, I would be glad.

Th: As you think about it, how do you suppose you would show it?

W: You never know if you ever please him.

Th: We have already discovered that you and Ralph have not yet developed crystal-clear ways of showing value feelings toward one another. Maybe you, Alice, are now observing this between Jim and Ralph. What do think, Ralph? Do you suppose it would be hard for Jim to find out when he has pleased you?

14. The therapist will not only exemplify what he means by clear communication, but he will teach his patients how to achieve it themselves.

   a. He will spell out the rules for communication accurately. In particular, he will emphasize the necessity for checking out meaning *given* with meaning *received*. He will see that the patient keeps in mind the following complicated set of mirror images:
   — Self's idea (how I see me).
   — Self's idea of other (how I see you).

— Self's idea of other's idea of self (how I see you seeing me).

— Self's idea of other's idea of self's idea of other (how I see you seeing me seeing you).

Only if a person is able to check back and forth across the lines of communication, can he be sure that he has completed a clear exchange.

b. The therapist will help the patient to be aware of messages that are incongruent, confused or covert (see pages 173–174 for examples).

c. At the same time, the therapist will show the patient how to check on invalid assumptions that are used as fact. He knows that members of dysfunctional families are afraid to question each other to find out what each really means. They seem to say to each other: "I can't let you know what I see and hear and think and feel or you will drop dead, attack or desert me." As a result, each operates from his assumptions, which he takes from the other person's manifestations and thereupon treats as fact. The therapist uses various questions to ferret out these invalid assumptions, such as:

"What did you say? What did you hear me say?"

"What did you see or hear that led you to make that conclusion?"

"What message did you intend to get across?"

"If I had been there, what would I have seen or heard?"

"How do you know? How can you find out?"

"You look calm, but how do you feel in the stomach?"

d. Like any good teacher, the therapist will try to be crystal-clear.

— He will repeat, restate and emphasize his own observations, sometimes to the point of seeming repetitious and simple. He will do the same with observations made by members of the family.

— He will also be careful to give his reasons for arriving at any conclusion. If the patient is baffled by some statement of the therapist's and does not know the reasoning behind it, this will only increase his feelings of powerlessness.

15. The therapist will be aware of the many possibilities of interaction in therapy.

    a.   In the therapeutic situation, the presence of the therapist adds as many dyads (two-person systems) as there are people in the family, since he relates to each member. The therapist, like the other people present, operates as a member of various dyads but also as the observer of other dyads. These shifts of position could be confusing to him and to the family. If, for example, he has taken someone's part, he should clearly state he is doing so.

    b.   The therapist clarifies the nature of interchanges made during therapy, but he has to select those that are representative since he can't possibly keep up with everything that is said. Luckily, family sequences are apt to be redundant, so one clarification may serve a number of exchanges.

    c.   Here is an illustration of the way the therapist isolates and underlines each exchange.
       — When the therapist states, "When you, Ralph, said you were angry, I noticed that you, Alice, had a frown on your face," this is an example of the therapist reporting himself as a monad ("I *see* you, Alice; I *hear* you, Ralph"), and reporting to Ralph and Alice as monads (the use of the word *you*, followed by the specific name). Then, by the therapist's use of the word *when*, he establishes that there is a connection between the husband's report and the wife's report, thus validating the presence of an interaction.
       — If the therapist then turns to the oldest son, Jim, and says, "What do you, Jim, make of what just happened between your mother and father?" the therapist is establishing Jim as an observer, since family

members may forget that they monitor each other's behavior.

— When Jim answers, everyone knows what his perception is. If it turns out that Jim's report does not fit what either Alice or Ralph intended, then there is an opportunity to find out what was intended, what was picked up by Jim, and why he interpreted it that way.

16. Labeling an illness is a part of therapy that a therapist must approach with particular care.

   a. A therapist, when he deals with a patient, is confronting a person who has been labeled by others or by himself as having emotional, physical or social disorders. To the non-therapeutic observer, the behavior which signals the presence of a disorder is usually labeled "stupid," "crazy," "sick" or "bad."

   b. The therapist will use other labels, like " mentally defective," "underachieving," "schizophrenic," "manic-depressive," "psychosomatic," "sociopathic." These are labels used by clinicians to describe behavior which is seen to be deviant: deviant from the rest of the person's character, deviant from the expectation of others, and deviant from the context in which the person finds himself.

   c. The observations made by clinicians over the years have been brought together under a standardized labeling system called the "psychiatric nomenclature." It is a method of shorthand used by clinicians to describe deviant behavior.

   d. These labels often presuppose an exact duplication of all the individuals so labeled. Over the years, each of the labels has been given an identity, with prognosis and treatment implications based on the dimensions of that identity.

   e. If a therapist has labeled a person "schizophrenic," for instance, he may have based his prognosis of that person on his ideas about schizophrenia, rather than on an observation of a person who, among other labels like

"human being," "Jim," "husband," "father," "chemist,"
has the label "schizophrenic."

f. But neither the clinician or any other person has the
    right to treat him only in terms of the label
    "schizophrenic" while losing sight of him as a total
    human being. No label is infallible, because no diagnosis
    is, but by identifying the person with the label, the
    therapist shuts his mind to the possibility of different
    interpretations which different evidence might point to.

g. The therapist must say to his patient, in effect: You are
    behaving now with behavior which I, as a clinician,
    label "schizophrenia." But this label only applies *at this
    time, in this place,* and *in this context.* Future times,
    places and contexts may show something quite different.

17. Let us close this discussion of the role of the therapist with a
    look at some of the specific advantages family therapy will
    have compared to individual or group therapy.

    a. In family therapy, the therapist will have a greater
        opportunity to observe objectively. In individual therapy,
        since there are only two people, the therapist is part of
        the interaction. It is hard for him to be impartial. In
        addition, he must sift out the patient's own reactions and
        feelings from those which might be a response to clues
        from the therapist himself.

    b. The family therapist will be able to get firsthand
        knowledge of the patient in two important areas.
        — By observing the individual in his family, the
          therapist can see where he is in terms of his present
          level of growth.
        — By observing a child in the family group, the therapist
          can find out how his functioning came to be
          handicapped. He can see for himself how the husband
          and wife relate to each other and how they relate to
          the child.
        — This kind of firsthand knowledge is not possible in
          individual therapy, or even in group therapy, where
          the individual is with members of his peer group and
          the kind of interaction that can be studied is limited
          to this single aspect.

18. As a therapist, I have found certain concepts useful, somewhat like measuring tools, in determining the nature and extent of dysfunction in a family.

    a. I make an analysis of the techniques used by each member of the family for *handling the presence of different-ness*. A person's reaction to different-ness is an index to his ability to adapt to growth and change. It also indicates what attitudes he will have toward other members of his family, and whether he will be able to express these attitudes directly or not.

      — The members of any family need to have ways to find out about and make room for their different-ness. This requires that each can report directly what he perceives about himself and the other, to himself and to the other.

      — Example: Janet misses her hatpin. She must say, "I need my hatpin (clear), which I am telling you, Betty, about, (direct), and it is the hatpin that I use for the only black hat I have (specific)." Not: "Why don't you leave my hat alone?" or "Isn't there something you want to tell me?" or going into Betty's room and turning things upsidedown (unclear, indirect, and unspecific).

      — As I have said before, when one of the partners in a marriage is confronted with a different-ness in the other that he did not expect, or that he did not know about, it is important that he treat this as an opportunity to explore and to understand rather than as a signal for war.

      — If the techniques for handling different-ness are based on determining who is right (war), or pretending that the different-ness does not exist (denial), then there is a potential for pathological behavior on the part of any member of the family, but particularly the children.

    b. I make what I call a *role function analysis* to find out whether the members of a family are covertly playing roles different from those which their position in the family demands that they play (see page 172).

      — If two people have entered a marriage with the hope of extending the self, each is in effect put in charge of the other, thus creating a kind of mutual parasitic relationship.

— This relationship will eventually be translated into something that looks like a parent-child relationship. The adults, labeled "husband" and "wife," may in reality be functioning as mother and son, father and daughter, or as siblings, to the confusion of the rest of the family and, ultimately, themselves.

— Here is an oversimplified example of the way things might go in such a family:

> Suppose Mary takes over the role of sole parent, with Joe acting the part of her child. Joe then takes the part of a brother to their two children, John and Patty, and becomes a rival with them for their mother's affections. To handle his rivalry and prove his place, he may start drinking excessively, or he may bury himself in his work in order to avoid coming home. Mary, deserted, may turn to John in such a way as to make him feel he must take his father's place. Wishing to do so but in reality unable to, John may become delinquent, turning against his mother and choosing someone on the outside. Or he may accept his mother's invitation, which would be to give up being male and become homosexual. Patty may regress or remain infantile to keep her place. Joe may get ulcers. Mary may become psychotic.

— These are only some of the possibilities for disturbance in a family that has become dislocated by incongruent role-playing.

c. I make a *self-manifestation analysis* for each member of a family. If what a person says does not fit with the way he looks, sounds and acts, or if he reports his wishes and feelings as belonging to someone else or as coming from somewhere else, I know that he will not be able to produce reliable clues for any other person interacting with him. When such behavior, which I call *"manifesting incongruency,"* is present in the members of a family to any large degree, there will be a potential for development of pathology.

d. In order to find out how the early life of each member of a family has affected his present ways of behaving, I make what I call a *model analysis* (see pages 171–172).

— This means that I try to discover who the models were (or are) that influenced each family member in his early life; who gave him messages about the presence and desirability of growth; who gave him the blueprint from which he learned to evaluate and act on new experience; who showed him how to become close to others.

— Because these messages have survival significance, the ways in which they are given will automatically determine the way the individual interprets later messages from other adults, who may not be survival-connected but who may be invested with survival significance, like spouses, in-laws or bosses.*

19. The ideas in this chapter have been discussed out of the context of ongoing therapy, where they belong. In the next three chapters, I hope to show very specifically how I, as a therapist, incorporate them into the action of therapy, from the first time I see a family to the termination of treatment.

---

*While there are obvious connections between this theory and both the analytic concept of transference and the Sullivanian concept of parataxic distortion, there are also differences. In particular, instead of inferring from the transference the probable nature of the individual's early environment, I use the information about his past to evaluate the survival significance of his current messages.

CHAPTER XI

Opening Treatment

1. I should like to go behind the scenes and describe in detail the techniques I have found most useful in practicing family therapy. Although I naturally believe in my own methods, and hope that others may find it helpful to read about them, I do not mean to imply that they are the last and only word in therapeutic procedure.

    This is because I feel strongly that each therapist must find his unique and individual way of practicing his craft. When he deals with patients, he should never sacrifice his particular flavor to some kind of professional, impersonal ideal. As you will see, wherever I could I have kept my own style of phrasing things (like asking "What hurts?" of a family), my favorite idioms and ways of joking.

    I have also found that an informal and individual manner helps to keep a therapeutic interview from resembling a funeral rite or a courtroom scene, and establishes an atmosphere which encourages hopefulness and good will.

    In this section I have included examples of the kind of questions that I use to draw people out and make them aware of their own communication. These may seem unnecessarily repetitious and simple at times, or even as if

137

the therapist were hard of hearing. However, we must remember that when we are dealing with more than one person, and when these persons do not yet know how to say what they mean, or to ask what others mean, this repetitiousness and simplifying is a central part of the therapeutic process. It is often astonishing to an inexperienced therapist how frequently family members cannot ask even simple, fact-finding questions of each other and must be shown how.

Another reason for asking so many questions and repeating them for each person in the family, is to give the other persons present a new and perhaps enlightening perspective on the way things look, or looked, to the speaker.

2. Let us start now with the first contact the therapist has with a family member, which will probably be a telephone call. In this first contact, the therapist will concentrate on four things:

    a. He will try to find out who makes up the Jones family.
        — For example, does Johnny have brothers or sisters? If so, how old are they? Does grandmother live right around the corner? If so, how often is she involved in family life?
        — Has anyone recently moved in or out of the family? If so, who? Grandfather? A new baby? A boarder?

    b. He will try to find out the ages of family members, because such information tells him where all members are expected to be in their chronological maturity. It also tells him what kind of parenting load the mates have to carry.
        — For example, are Mary and her husband, Joe, in their twenties, thirties, fifties? Is this a young or an older family?
        — How old is Johnny? Where is he now in his growth toward maturity? (The therapist may not find out all these things in the first contact, but he keeps these questions in mind as he talks to Mary Jones on the phone.)

    c. He introduces Mary Jones to the family therapy approach, making it clear to her that it is important that her husband take part in the therapy.

d. Initially, he talks to Mary about herself and Joe as
    parents of Johnny, rather than as mates to each other. In
    this way he joins temporarily in their focus on Johnny as
    the problem; as "the reason why we have decided to ask
    for help."

e. Here is an example of a first contact on the phone:

> W: This is Mrs. Jones. I have heard about this idea
>   of family therapy and wondered if you could
>   help us.
>
> Th: What seems to be the problem?
>
> W: Well, we are having problems with my boy,
>   Johnny. He is not doing at all well in school. As
>   a matter of fact he . . . he has not been a very
>   difficult child at all up to now. But he has this
>   new teacher who has been pretty hard on him. I
>   don't know. He just won't behave, and we have
>   received several complaints from the school.
>   They say he is quite tense, and I guess he is . . .
>
> Th: I see. The teachers have complained about
>   Johnny's behavior in school. He is tense. How
>   does he show this? How do they say he shows
>   this?
>
> W: Well, he cuts up a good deal and won't settle
>   down, and they say he is hard to handle. I just
>   don't understand it. Frankly, I'm at my wits' end.
>   He won't tell me what is wrong, and I thought
>   maybe if you would . . . if there is something we
>   are doing wrong . . .
>
> Th: It certainly sounds as if things aren't going as
>   you hoped. We can look at this and see how it
>   came about and try to understand it better.
>
> W: Well, we have done everything we could. We
>   have given him everything a child could want.
>
> Th: I'm sure this has been confusing to you, and you
>   are trying hard to make some sense of it. As you
>   know, we do family work here, and I think we
>   should start out with you and your husband. I

think that would be best. You are the adults in the family. Tell me, who is in your family?

W: Well, there's Johnny and Patty. And my husband, Joe, and me. Just four of us.

Th: There are four of you. Your husband's name is Joe. And Johnny and Patty, what are their ages?

W: Johnny is ten. Patty is going on seven.

Th: Johnny is ten. Patty is almost seven. Anyone else in the family?

W: No.

Th: Well, as I said, we do family work here. So we should start out with the two adults. I would be happy to make an appointment for you and your husband. Then later we can see about bringing the children in.

W: Well, I . . . well, I'm not sure. Joe would . . . I'm not sure he would want to do that. I haven't asked him but he's . . .

Th: We need information from your husband that only he can give. It is very important that I see you both. Tell your husband that a family is not a family without the father and the mother present. It is very important that we have the opportunity to get his contributions on this.

W: Well, I'll tell him. But I don't know. He's pretty . . . he's not too sympathetic . . . He's, uh . . .

Th: Tell your husband that we need his contributions. We need to get his view of the situation as the male adult in the family. We need all the information we can get, and a father's contributions are very important. Only he can speak for himself. No one else can give what he can give.

W: Well, I'll try. When could you see us?

Joe will come in with his wife for the first appointment. Rarely, with this kind of approach, does the husband, in his role of father, fail to respond. The therapist's emphasis seems to give the husband a new importance in the wife's eyes.

3. In the first interview, the therapist will start out by asking questions to establish what the family wants and expects from treatment.

    a. He will ask each person present, though not necessarily in these words:

> "How did you happen to come here?"
>
> "What do you expect will happen here?"
>
> "What do you hope to accomplish here?"

    b. The therapist will then explain the nature of family therapy. He may say:

> "Families operate by rules which they may not even know about. I want to know about the operation of this family."
>
> "Each member of a family has to do something when he sees the presence of pain in another member. I need to find out what each of you does."
>
> "No one person can see the whole picture because he is limited to his own perspective. By having everyone together we can get the whole picture more clearly. Every person has a unique contribution to make which cannot be duplicated by anyone else."

    c. The therapist will then ask each member of the family some questions for finding out about the symptom and its meaning such as:

> "Tell me, what do *you* see as the pain in this family?"

"Anyone with a problem has pain in some way.
Can you tell me where the pain is?"

"What 'hurts' in this family?"

Any one of these questions introduces the idea that the
family, as a family, does have pain. It starts to shift the
focus from the Identified Patient to the family as a
whole. Each family member has a chance to identify, for
himself, the problem area.

d. The parents usually answer that the Identified Patient is
the problem and the therapist *briefly* orients himself to
the problem as the parents see it:

"When did you first notice this symptom?"

"Did you discuss it between yourselves?"

"What steps did you take to try and relieve it?"

"What happened to these attempts?"

These questions allow the parents to tell how they have
tried to be good parents and to present themselves
accurately as puzzled. These questions also help the
therapist get his first clues on several things: Who speaks
for whom? Who makes the family rules? Who makes the
plans? Who carries them out? How clearly are the plans
communicated? Who speaks the most? Who speaks the
least? What is the general pacing and tone of family
communication? How clear and direct is family
communication? How does the family respond to crises?
In what area of behavior is the symptom manifested
(I.Q., body, emotions, social)? What were the
circumstances surrounding the onset of the symptom?
What gap existed between onset and labeling of the
symptom? Who (or what) has been blamed for the
existence of the symptom (neighbors, teachers, God,
heredity)? What purpose does the symptom serve in the
family?

e. The therapist decreases threat of blame by accentuating
the idea of puzzlement and the idea of good intentions:

"This must have puzzled you, that you did all these things and still nothing seemed to turn out as you hoped."

"We are all human. We do the best we can. It must have confused you when, with all these efforts, nothing seemed to go right."

f. The therapist then makes a bridge in order to cross over to beginning the family study. He may say:

"It sounds as though you have all been puzzled as to how this difficulty of yours came to be."

"Once no one in this room knew each other. Maybe that time is hard to remember, and it may seem that you have always known each other. That is not so. You came together one by one. Each time another came, the others already there had to work out ways to make room for the new one."

"Now let's see who the persons are who have made up this family."

CHAPTER XII

Using a Family Life Chronology

---

1. When I look at a family, I see three different generations.

   a. In my mind, I see the parents as children, living and growing up with their parents (who are now the grandparents), learning both implicit and explicit rules on how to approach life.

   b. I see the parents as architects of their present family. They bring together what they have learned in their own families, blending it both consciously and unconsciously to form the context of their current family.

   c. The third family is an actuality if there are married children. If not, the "third family" is a future family built on the child's current experience of the present family. In any case, the children are learning how to become adults, whether or not they form a family.

2. This means the family is made up of parents, grandparents, and children. Each generation represents a different context at a different time and place. The circumstances, context, and the time at which this current family comes together (and in which its members have moved in and out) is the

territory that I used as my basis for the discovery of the evolvement of this particular family.

    a.   Each family has a unique history with its own meanings and interpretations to each of its members.

    b.   Each family has its own set of explicit and implicit rules about how to approach life. A look at any three-generational family will quickly show how these implicit and explicit rules have been woven into the current fabric of their family life:
— directly
— by obviously ignoring their existence, projecting the rules onto something else
— by denying their existence and doing the opposite
— by distorting the rules in some way, or
— by comfortably discarding the rules altogether.

3. The family therapist enters a session knowing little or nothing specific about the family.

    a.   One might know who the Identified Patient is and what symptoms are manifested, but that is usually all. Getting clues about the meaning of the symptom in that family system will be the beginning of the exploration.

    b.   One might suspect that pain exists in the marital relationship. It is important to find out how the pain shows itself. One needs to explore how the mates have tried to cope with their problems.

    c.   The family therapist will know that the mates both operate largely from "models" derived from what they saw going on (or not going on) between their own parents. It is necessary to find out how these models have influenced each mate's expectations about how to be a mate and how to be a parent.

4. The family therapist enters a session knowing that the family has had a history. The family life chronology is essentially a history of the events that took place in both the inner and external worlds of the family. It also reveals how family members interpreted and responded to these events.

a. Examples of inner family events are: the birth or death of a child, or the divorce or death of a parent, or a grandparent moving in with or out from the family.

b. Examples of an external world event are: a war, an economic depression, a rigid new law, or a marked change in the family's economic status (either higher or lower).

c. When there have been a lot of fragmentations and distractions within the family over many years, structuring a chronology very often helps the family therapist to get a perspective on the family.

5. One of the main things the family therapist needs to find out is how people coped with whatever happened.

a. How someone copes is a function of his or her self-esteem. It also gives clues to the implicit emotional rules in the family.

b. Having a chronology of the events at time and place allows the therapist a "feel" of the real journey this family took.

6. The way in which I handle getting historical information is by emphasizing my appreciation of each person's method of coping and of what they coped with.

a. I discoverd long ago that people are always doing the best they know how to do at the time, although it may not be the best in hindsight or from an observor's point of view.

b. Whatever a person is doing represents what he pays attention to, how he experiences that, how he interprets it, and what actions he associates with that interpretation.

c. This constitutes the whole direction of what goes into coping. Changing how and what one looks at, seeing new possibilities and interpretations, and discovering various options will automatically lead one to a new coping.

7. Family members enter therapy with a great deal of fear.

   a. Family members are often covertly feeling to blame for the fact that "nothing" seems to have turned out right (even though they may overtly blame the Identified Patient or the other mate).

   b. Parents especially need to feel that they did the best they could as parents. They need to tell the therapist: "This is why I did what I did. This is what happened to me."

   c. A family life chronology that deals with facts such as names, dates, labeled relationships, moves, etc., seems to appeal to the family. It asks questions that members can answer, questions that are relatively nonthreatening. It deals with life as the family understands it.

8. I used to take this chronology in a fairly rigid way. Now I spend more time initially making contact in the here and now with family members.

   a. After the initial contact is made between family members and myself, I draw a map on the blackboard. This is simply a way of finding out who was in the family when.

   b. Sorting out factual information about the presence and absence of family members seems to be less threatening at this early stage that if it is done later. At this early stage, making the map can be compared to asking about one's health and vital signs. Since it is factual information, the chronology can be given without too much emotional import.

   c. In this informational, fact-gathering manner, the family therapist can get most of the clues that help to understand the family process: Whose father is who? If there is a second wife, where is the mother of the children? etc.

   d. The therapist should watch the responses of other family members as people give information. These reactions can be filed for future reference, or the therapist may utilize them further as they arise.

9. By the time I finish drawing the map, I have particularized this family. I have also responded to the factual information. I have modeled an experience in nonblame.

   a. As an example, I learn that the man in front of me is the stepfather. Then I ask: "Which of the children here did you bring with you into the marriage?" That leaves room for me to ask the child in question, "Oh, you're thirteen now. How long have you been in this new family?" This question carries the implied message that this child had a new experience. The emphasis is not on the kind of experience but only that there was one.

   b. I might also inquire as to where the mother is. Or I might ask the child: "How is it working out—getting yourself a new mothering person?" With a few well-placed questions of this sort, I can penetrate to the heart of the family matter.

   c. If I find that one of the people present is a grandmother who entered this family two weeks ago after the death of her husband, I will know that grieving is going on somewhere. That grieving means something for the parent whose father died, for the children whose grandfather died, and for the woman who lost her husband.
      — If the Identified Patient in the family at this point is a child, I might casually inquire how things were between that child and the grandparent.
      — So that it does not become too pointed, I might ask the same question of other members of the family.

10. The family therapist needs to judge how much attention is given to any one part of the chronology.

    a. The goal is to get a perspective and to provide one for the family.

    b. The therapist needs to keep a keen eye out for the coping processes that the family members are using as they relate their histories.

    c. The therapist should also keep in mind certain general characteristics of families in therapy. The following

represent some special awarenesses I have as I work my
way into discovering the family with which I am
working.

d. Family members enter therapy with a great deal of
    despair. Therapist structuring helps stimulate hope.
    — As far as family members are concerned, past events
      are part of them. They now can tell the therapist: "I
      existed." And they can also tell him: "I am not just a
      big blob of pathology. I succeeded in overcoming
      many handicaps."
    — If the family knew what questions needed asking they
      wouldn't need to be in therapy. So the therapist does
      not say: "Tell me what you want to tell me." Family
      members will simply tell the therapist what they have
      been telling themselves for years. The therapist's
      questions say: "I know what to ask. I take
      responsibility for understanding you. We are going to
      go somewhere."

e. The family therapist also knows that, to some degree, the
    family has focused on an Identified Patient in order to
    relieve marital pain. He also knows that, to some degree,
    the family will resist any effort to change this focus. A
    family life chronology is an effective, nonthreatening
    way to change from an emphasis on the "sick" or "bad"
    family member to an emphasis on the marital
    relationship.

f. The family life chronology serves other useful therapy
    purposes, such as providing the framework within which
    a re-education process can take place. As we have said,
    the therapist serves as a model in the way he checks out
    information or corrects communication techniques, and
    the way he places his questions and elicits answers can
    allow him to begin this process. In addition, when he
    takes the chronology, he can introduce in a relatively
    nonfrightening way some of the crucial concepts by
    which he hopes to induce change.

11. From the family life chronology, the therapist gets his first
    clues as to how dysfunctional the marital relationship is.

    a. If, for example, while answering the therapist's
        questions, the mates can readily talk about the pain in

their own marital relationship, the prognosis for an early, successful outcome in therapy is good.

b. But if, during the chronology, the mates cannot readily talk about the marital relationship but insist on focusing on the Identified Patient and on themselves as parents of a sick or bad child, the prognosis for an early, successful outcome in therapy is not as good.

c. Also, if the child (the I. P.) helps the parents to keep the focus on himself (schizophrenics and delinquents do this), the therapist has the extra task of trying to reassure the I. P. that it is safe to talk about the pain between his parents, while at the same time reassuring the mates.

12. Family therapy is, in one sense, a form of marital therapy, even though the family therapist also deals with the mates in their parental roles.

a. But how the therapist deals with the parental role depends on the age of the children. As I see it, the parental role only exists in relation to children who are still in the family and not yet of age. After a child is twenty-one, he must be treated as another adult, because this is the reality he and his parents must be educated to accept if they have not yet been able to do so (see page 136).

b. Family therapy must be focused primarily on the mates as mates because their marital pain has prevented them from parenting their child according to his growth needs. They have parented him according to their needs.

c. Family therapy must be focused primarily on the mates as mates because their marital pain is what the Identified Patient and all other children in the family are most acutely attuned to and affected by.
    — Parents who are unhappy with each other cannot give a child a feeling that his home base is secure.
    — Nor can they be helpful models for the child of what a comfortable, rewarding male-female relationship is like.

13. Once the therapist has briefly dealt with the problem as the family defines it, he then starts with the chronology, commencing with the mates.*

    a. The mates were around first; they are, in fact, the architects of the family.
        — By dealing first with the mates, the therapist also starts to delineate the marital relationship.
        — He also helps the child to see his parents as people who had lives long before he was born.

    b. He starts with the mates, even though the family, as a family, did not begin to exist until the arrival of the first child. If he started with each parent's relationship to his child, he would be putting the cart before the horse.

14. The nucleus of the later family group began to exist when the mates first laid eyes on each other and decided to continue the relationship.

    a. At this stage, the basic marital homeostasis (or definition of relationship) began to be formed. So any chronology must begin at this first meeting between the two future mates.

    b. The male and female who decided to continue the relationship may have spent some time forming one before they got married. So any chronology must cover the period between the first meeting and marriage.

    c. The male and female who became mates probably lived together for a while as a childless couple. So any chronology must cover the period before the mates took on the parental role.

    d. Also, both mates had, themselves, grown up in a family. So any chronology must include some picture of what

---

*As he does this, the therapist may take notes, either to refresh his own memory, for research purposes, or to show the family that he takes their history seriously. On the other hand, many therapists will tape interviews or will find note-taking disruptive. This, since Freud's early remarks on the matter, remains an individual problem.

life was like in both original family environments.
(Although this information belongs chronologically first,
the therapist must be present-family oriented, so he
starts with the period when the mates first met each
other; he starts with the beginning of the *present*
family.)

15. Before going into the actual questions the therapist can ask
and the order in which he can ask them, let me emphasize
the manner, spirit, or style in which the therapist must ask
his questions.

   a. The family therapist takes the family life chronology in
   a casual yet attentive way (see page 161).

   b. He behaves as though he were a family chronicler, out
   collecting facts on family life. He does this in an
   atmosphere of hopeful discovery; the family and he
   together are going to paint a picture of the past. All
   members will have perceptions of events to offer, even
   though one person's perceptions may not jibe with those
   of another.

   c. He does not behave like a census taker, a funeral
   director, or a district attorney interrogating the accused.
   He and the family are scientists, working together on a
   task. For example, the therapist can say:

      "Then Grandma comes back into the picture. Is
      that right? When did that happen, as you remember
      it? Before or after Suzie, here, came on the scene?"

16. The therapist first gets what I call a Cast of Characters, as if
he were orienting himself to a drama:

      "Well, now, to get a fuller picture of this, tell me
      who is in your family."

      "What are the names of your children? Where are
      they now? What are their ages?"

It is wise to remember that there may be other children in
the family besides those present in the therapy room.

17. If the therapist finds that one or both mates had previous marriages, he pauses to ask for names, ages, whereabouts of previous mate and children from previous marriages. He also asks for date of previous marriage, date of divorce from or death of previous mate.

> "I see. Then you have been married before. Then this is a family made up of some children from that previous marriage."

> "When did you first marry?"

> "What led to the separation?"

Often the father in the therapy room is really a stepfather or an adoptive father. Such questions about the Cast of Characters quickly reveal possible problem areas in the present family.

18. The therapist finds out if any other people are presently living with the family, people such as in-laws, boarders, aunts, etc. He also asks about any persons *not* still in the family who have received or contributed nurture, financial support or direction (guidance-discipline) in the past.

> "Are there any other people living with you now?"

> "Are there any other persons who at any time in the past have been members of this family?"

> "When did each come into the family?"

> "What was the reason that each joined the family?"

> "Where did each come from?"

> "When did each leave the family?"

> "What was the reason for leaving the family?"

> "Where did each go?"

> "Where is each of these persons now?"

> "What is the contact between each of these persons and each of the present family members now?"

> "I see, then we have all the people who were or are part of this family."

By constantly repeating the idea of "this family," the therapist helps the family (especially the parents) to see that they are, in fact, a unique unit. Also, by checking on the whereabouts of all family members, the therapist may discover that a daughter is in a mental hospital nearby and one mate's parents live right around the corner. In other words, many people who are not in the therapy room may be very much in the picture. The therapist must know about them.

19. The therapist then defines the therapy task, giving his own orientation:

> "As you know, we work with families here. And we have found that when one member has pain, all share this pain in some way. Our task is to work out ways in which everyone can get more pleasure from family life. Because I am sure that at one time this family had better times."

By speaking in general, the therapist prevents any specific member from feeling responsible for the unhappiness in the family.

Also, by accentuating the idea of pleasure as the goal of therapy, the therapist continues to decrease fear and increase hope.

Finally, by talking about "what we see" in families, the therapist uses his special knowledge about families in order to help family members to see themselves as not *especially* bad or hopeless.

20. The therapist then shifts to the mates as the leaders of the family:

"Well, now, you two haven't been parents all your
lives. You knew each other long before 'this one'
(the I. P.) came along. Tell me, how did you two
happen to choose each other as mates?"

By shifting to an earlier period in order to approach the
marital relationship, the therapist continues to decrease
threat. The period he is asking about is when both mates felt
more hopeful than at present. And, with follow-up questions,
the therapist continues to expand information on earlier
expectations:

"What was it about her that led you to say, 'She's
for me'?"

"Well, there must have been other fellows at the
dance, too. Why this one in particular?"

21. The therapist asks about steps taken to continue the
relationship:

"So when did you meet again? Who took that
important next step? How did it come about?"

"So he called you up. What did you do? Did you
expect him to do this? What did you expect her to
do?"

"And then what happened?"

"When did you both agree that you wanted to
continue the relationship?"

"When did you two announce to the world that you
were serious about your courting?"

The two mates usually get quickly involved talking about
this almost-forgotten time. And the child, left in the
appropriate role of observer, has an opportunity to see his
parents as two people who lived before he did and once had
a happier relationship with each other.

Questions about this period also continue to delineate the
mates *as mates,* and each mate as an individual who has
made a decision to live with the other in marriage. The

effect of these questions on the mates seems to be: "We *were* happy once. We can be again." The effect of these questions on the child seems to be: "My parents were *happy* once. Maybe they can be again."

22. The therapist turns to the child (or I. P.) repeatedly during this meeting-and-marriage story, and asks him if he knew about this period of his parents' lives:

> "Maybe it's hard to believe that at one time your parents didn't even know each other."

> "Did you know this about Dad? That he was struggling to earn enough money so he could marry your Mother?"

> "Did you know that your Mother thought so little of herself that she believed no man would want to marry her?"

Even if the child refuses to answer the therapist, these questions still continue. By speaking to the child in front of his parents (an "aside"), the therapist can begin to give interpretations not only to the child but indirectly to his parents. He starts communicating his view of their "worthwhileness" at the same time that he takes the chronology.

23. The therapist asks about the decision and plans for the marriage:

> "When did you decide to marry? How did you go about making plans to marry?"

> "What was the marriage ceremony like? Who was there?"

> "What obstacles stood between you and marriage?"

These questions bring out realistic details about income, war, job changes, death or illness of parents, etc. They also emphasize the idea that both mates chose each other; their marriage did not just happen.

The questions also bring out problems which either or both mates had in separating from, yet trying to please, their own parents. (For example, you often find out that the mates went through two marriage ceremonies in order to please their parents.)

These questions also give the I. P. a coherent story about the natural development of the family. This unraveling of the past helps undistort reality.

24. The therapist asks for each mate's idea of the other mate's response when the decision to marry came up:

> "When was the idea of marriage first talked about? In what context? How was the idea communicated? What was said? Who first mentioned it?"

> "What was your (husband's) picture of your wife's response?"

> "What was your (wife's) picture then of your husband's response?"

> "What were you (wife) thinking and feeling when your husband asked you to marry him? What did you (husband) feel?"

25. If there are discrepancies in the two pictures, the therapist tries to reveal and interpret them. He uses this instance to begin introducing the couple to the idea that they may be operating from an insufficient understanding of each other and that there are ways to correct such misunderstandings. He states:

> "You (wife) were feeling and thinking something different from what your husband thought you were feeling and thinking."

> "How do you explain that your husband got a picture about what you were feeling and thinking that was different from what you actually were feeling and thinking?"

"How do you (husband) explain that you got a different picture from that which your wife was feeling and thinking and from what you intended?"

"Does this situation ever occur in the reverse, that is, that you (wife) get a different picture from what you (husband) intend?"

"What happens when either of you sees that each of you somehow has not gotten the other's message? *This of course happens to everyone. Everyone needs techniques to handle this.*"

"What happens when each of you turns up with different pictures of presumably the same thing?"

"What techniques do you know about that you (wife) and you (husband) have developed to handle this situation?"

"This could sometimes look as if someone were lying, or that they were bad, stupid, sick, or crazy."

"I think this is an area where we need to do some work. Now let's get back!"

26. The therapist then asks about parental reactions to the decision to marry:

"How did your parents react to your courting and decision to marry?"

"Where were your parents living at the time? Where were you living at the time?"

These questions naturally lead to information about each mate's relationship with his or her own parents. Usually this area is emotionally loaded and also leads to early marital conflicts.

The therapist gears the chronology to the responses he receives from the family. If one or both mates show an interest in discussing their premarital lives, the therapist pauses in his chronology of events in the nuclear family and now concentrates on the chronology of each mate's life in his family of origin. Such a diversion further delineates each mate as an individual with a separate premarital life of his own.

27. The therapist then goes further into the relations between the engaged pair and their future in-laws. He directs the following series of questions to the wife and repeats them for the husband:

> "What did you (wife) know about how your father felt about your marrying your husband? How did you know this?"

> "What did you know about how your mother felt about your marrying your husband? How did you know this?"

> "What did you know about how your husband's mother felt about having you for a daughter-in-law? How did you come to know this?"

> "How did you know about how your husband's father felt about having you for a daughter-in-law?"

> "Did you (husband) have the same impression as your wife?" (If different, the therapist will label the fact that there is a difference and what the difference is.)

> "How do you account for the difference in your impressions?"

28. The therapist goes on to ask about the couple's present relations with their in-laws:

> "How are things now between you (wife) and your mother-in-law, your father-in-law, your mother, your father?"

> "How are things now between you (husband) and your mother, your father, your father-in-law, your mother-in-law?"

"How would you like things to be different?"

29. The therapist now expands the Cast of Characters to include each mate's brothers, sisters, mother, father, aunt, etc.

> "Both of you came from your own family environments. We'd better get a picture of who is in these families."
>
> "Do you have brothers and sisters? How old are they? Younger or older than you?"
>
> "Then that makes you the eldest in the family."
>
> "What are their names? Where are they living now? Are they married? Do they have children? How old are their children?"
>
> "Where are your parents living now? How old are they? What does your father do for a living?"

Because this area is usually loaded, the therapist first concentrates on facts: names, ages, sex, whereabouts of family members. In this way he gets a picture of what each mate's family environment must have been like. He puts off details about relationships and feelings until he has some loose framework to fit them in. He does not encourage a family member to wallow in feelings until he has some idea what the feelings may be about. He constantly relates feelings and perceptions to time, place and context.

These questions about each mate's pre-marital environment also give the therapist clues as to what people in the extended family, or family of origin, have been influential in the lives of the people in the nuclear family. These questions also show the present geographical spread and cluster of all these influential people.

30. After expanding the Cast of Characters to include the two families of origin, the therapist asks each mate to describe his two parents.

> "If I were to meet your (husband's) mother in a railroad station, how would I recognize her? How would I know your father?"

> "If I had the opportunity to talk to your (wife's) mother, what would she tell me about how food, money, sex, discussion of children and fun were handled in your family? What would your father tell me?"

By asking perceptual questions, the therapist can help each mate give information about his relationship to his parents without calling up anxiety. And the therapist can receive more clues on the models from which both mates are operating.

31. As he concentrates on each mate's relationship to his own parents, the therapist can introduce several new concepts into the family ideology, and introduce them in the least threatening way, since they are one step removed from the nuclear family. Here he introduces the concept that people are different. He says, to each mate in turn:

> "I noticed as you were talking that your mother and father were alike in these ways, and different in these ways." (And he labels the differences.)

> "How did you see them manage to live with these differences?"

32. Different-ness is a loaded idea in dysfunctional families. By reminding the mates that they were children once, observing their parents as different, the therapist begins to introduce the idea that their child sees them as different. That it is all right to be different. The therapist can say:

> *"Everyone needs ways to handle the presence of differences.* It looks as if in your (wife's) family it was handled like this. In your (husband's) family it was handled like this."

> "How do you (wife) see yourself as *like* your husband?"

"How do you see yourself as *different* from your husband?"

"How do you (husband) see yourself as like your wife?"

"How do you see yourself as different from your wife?"

"What ways have you each worked out to live with your differences from each other?"

"How do these ways work out?"

33. The therapist concludes by pointing out the unsuitability of the husband's, or wife's, ways of handling different-ness:

"It looks as if you both have been trying to use the same ways that your parents used."

"Of course, you (wife) are like no one else and you (husband) are like no one else. All people are different. No one exactly duplicates anyone else."

"It looks as if the ways you are using fitted your parents all right, in their time and place, but they don't fit *you*—we need to find ways that fit you as you both are."

"Perhaps, without your knowing it, you (husband) have been behaving toward your wife as though she were your mother, and you (wife) have been behaving toward your husband as though he were your father."

"Perhaps, without knowing it, you (husband) have been expecting your wife to respond like your mother and have behaved toward her accordingly. And you (wife) may have expected your husband to respond to you like your father and so you behaved toward him accordingly."

"Our parents are our first teachers. We get our ideas of how to behave from what we see, what we

*experience and what we are told, and all this
comes to us from our first teachers. You got your
ideas from your respective first teachers."*

34. The therapist introduces the idea that people disagree. He
asks each mate:

> "Of course everyone disagrees at times. Were your
> mother and father able to disagree openly?"

> "How did you see your mother and father go about
> disagreeing?"

Both mates still suffer from varying degrees of prohibition
against commenting on pain which they saw existing
between their own parents. The therapist not only receives
clues on the degree of the prohibition but also begins to
relieve the mates of it.

35. The therapist introduces the idea that pain can be looked at
and commented on (see page 167):

> "Did you see your parents' pain?"

> "Were you able to relieve their pain?"

> "How did you go about it?"

> "How did Mother respond when you tried to help?"

> "How did Father respond when you tried to help?"

These questions continue to remind the mates that they were
children once, observing their own parents. A dysfunctional
parent has difficulty seeing the child as the child is. The
therapist begins to stimulate this awareness by reminding
the parent of how *he* felt as a child, by helping the parent to
step, temporarily, back into the child's shoes. But he
stimulates this awareness where it is safe, one step removed
from the present nuclear family.

36. The therapist introduces the idea that people can have fun:

"What did your parents do for fun?"

Dysfunctional people have as much trouble talking about pleasure as they have talking about pain.

37. The therapist, in eliciting information about each mate's premarital life, helps highlight discrepancies between what the parents did and what they told their children to do:

> "How did you (wife) see your mother treat your father?"
>
> "How did you see your mother treat you?"
>
> "How did your mother tell you to treat your father?"
>
> "How have you explained the difference?"

The therapist repeats these questions to the husband. These questions indirectly show the mates the kinds of questions their child may be asking of them.

38. The therapist, in eliciting information about each mate's premarital environment, shows that family events affect different members:

> "So your father lost his job just about the time you were hoping to go to college? How did the family cope with this problem?"

39. The therapist, in eliciting information from each mate, tries to weave back and forth between the mates in order to keep the information at the same time and developmental period:

> "Let's see, then, by the time you had managed to get yourself to college your wife, here, must have started high school. Let's find out how she got herself up to this period."

40. The therapist also compares one mate's experience with the other mate's experience:

"Well, now, evidently you (husband) saw your father leave the house when he and your mother disagreed. What did you (wife) see your father doing?"

"I gather that things in your (husband's) house seemed pained but quiet whereas in your (wife's) house people were fighting openly all the time. Am I right?"

41. Sometimes one mate's premarital story will be extensive and productive for therapy, so the therapist continues to concentrate on that mate. If so, he turns to the other mate and says:

"We'll have to get to you next time, I guess, and find out how things were going for you during this period."

In effect, the therapist says: "There *is* enough to go around. Everyone will have the chance to tell his story. Everyone will be included in therapy."

42. The therapist brings both mates' chronology up to the time of marriage. He then accentuates the idea that people are influenced by past models. And he asks for information on how the mates translated what they had learned:

"Well, now, we have some idea of each of your models. Let's see how these growing-up experiences influenced how you two went about being married."

First he asks the mates what plans for their future life were made at the time of their marriage, and what ideas they had about it:

"Where were you planning to live?"

"What were the plans for how the two of you would be supported?"

"What were the plans about how you were going to divide household tasks?"

"What were the plans for handling, distributing, and spending money?"

"What arrangements had you made for quarreling and disagreeing, which everyone who is close to somebody else is bound to do from time to time?

"What arrangements had each of you made for the individual interests of the other?"

"What plans had you made for having children?"

"When did you plan to have a child or children?"

"How many did you want?"

"What sex children had you hoped for?"

"What plans had you made for having fun?"

"What did each of you think about where you would be, what you would be doing, and what you would look like ten years after the marriage? Twenty years after the marriage?"

43. Then the therapist asks what actually did take place. For example, he will ask about the early days of the marriage:

"Did you have a honeymoon? Where? How long? How did it go?"

"Where did you set up housekeeping?"

"Were either of you continuing schooling after you married?"

"Were you working? Where?"

"You went into the Army at that time? When was that? Before or after your mother moved in to live with you and your wife?"

The therapist keeps track of each person in terms of age as he moves through time from the marriage date to the

present. As each event comes along, he asks how it came to
be, who first mentioned the idea, and under what
circumstances. He finds out what the other thought and how
he responded to the idea. He ascertains who came into the
family, who left. The therapist uses these questions to create
a sequential picture of the past, cross-referring all
information. He also uses them to further delineate problem
areas and success areas. Often such questions don't have to
be asked; the mates will volunteer the answers.

44. The process of getting this information serves other therapy
purposes too.

a. By focusing on the mates when they were childless, the
therapist further accentuates the idea that the mates
have a relationship separate from the parental role.

b. Also, by emphasizing the influence of the past, he
continues to decrease blame and threat. He helps to
make past and present behavior look more
understandable.

45. The therapist asks each mate what he had expected from
marriage:

"What did you want your marriage to be like?" This
question helps the therapist find out what
distortions each mate would have to make in order
to explain away disappointment. For example, was
the wife looking primarily for a roof over her head?
Or for someone to comfort her? Or for the ice
cream she never had enough of as a child? Was the
husband looking primarily for enough to eat? For
uncritical devotion? For regularly darned socks?

46. The therapist checks out whether expectations, hopes, fears,
got communicated:

"Did you tell her this? That food was very
important to you? Did she know that you always
feared you might starve?"

"Did you tell him that a house had a special meaning for you?"

47. The therapist asks what things each mate particularly liked in the other and whether each had (and has) a clear way of expressing these feelings. He asks this of the husband (and then puts the same series of questions to the wife):

> "What things do you remember that you found pleasant and satisfying in your wife?"
>
> "Did you (wife) know that he thought these things about you?"
>
> "If you did, how did you come to find this out?"
>
> "If not, how do you (husband) explain that she did not know?"
>
> "Was it that you (wife) did not ask or that you (husband) did not tell?"
>
> "Do you (wife) know about his thoughts in regard to this now?"

48. The therapist brings up the concept of different-ness again, this time in a present-day context. He asks each mate what he did *not* like about the other mate and how he planned to deal with these disliked qualities. (The following questions are later redirected toward the other mate.)

> "What things do you remember finding out about each other that were unpleasant, new, different, or even bad? *There are always imperfections in people and each is different from the other.*"
>
> "Did you (husband) know that your wife felt this about you?"
>
> "If yes, how did you find out?"
>
> "If not, how did you (wife) explain that your husband did not know?"

> "What ways did you (wife) have in mind about coping with what you saw was unpleasant (or 'different' or 'bad') in him?"

> "How have these worked out?"

> "Do you (husband) know what your wife's thoughts are in regard to this now?"

49. The therapist points up discrepancies and asks the mates to explain how they have integrated them. The wife's nagging seemed protective before marriage. Now it is seen as domineering. The husband's forgetfulness seemed lovable before marriage. Now it is seen as irresponsible. Each thought that love and time would conquer all.

> "How have you explained it to yourself that some things you hoped for haven't worked out?"

> "How have you explained it to yourself that you need to have enough to eat yet chose a wife who hates to cook?"

> "How can it be that you need to feel secure by owning a house, yet you chose a husband who hates to stay in one place?"

These questions help the therapist find out how much the relationship was based on uncommunicated hopes rather than on communicated reality-testing. The therapist's comments, by highlighting the discrepancy between hopes and marital choice, also shows each mate that he had some responsibility for his marital choice.

50. The therapist explains discrepancies by referring to the models from each mate's past, and also by accentuating the need for clear communication:

> "I guess something else was going on here that led you to think you could not ask for what you wanted. Maybe you felt you had to crawl under the carpet like your mother."

"I guess you thought you had to please the ladies all the time. That's what you saw your dad doing. Maybe that's why you couldn't ask for what you wanted."

These statements continue to relate the past to the present. But they also imply that the past need not continue to influence the present and that people can free themselves from this influence.

51. The therapist continues the chronology to include plans for and arrival of each child. He also explores the physical circumstances at the time of birth. He repeats his questions for each child, since each child is a different experience in parenting. Usually the mates had only the barest notion of how parenting would affect their lives, especially of how it would affect their relationship as mates.

"When did you both decide to include parenting in your lives?"

"Which sex child had you hoped for first?" (to each)

"Where was this?"

"How did the birth go?" (to wife)

"Where were you?" (to husband)

"When did each of you decide you wanted to become a parent?"

"What do you suppose was the reason you wanted to become a parent at that particular time?" (to each)

"How long did it take after your decision before conception took place?"

"What do you suppose stood in the way?" (if it was a long period)

What kinds of changes did you think would come about when the baby came?" (to each)

Here the therapist brings in a "universal truth": "Changes always come when a baby comes," to suggest that the couple is not unusual in finding a new baby a strain. Then:

"How did you plan for these changes?" (to each)

"How have these plans worked out?"

"What kind of changes actually did come about for you?"

52. The therapist moves on to ask about the younger children, not forgetting that there may also be other children by an earlier marriage, now living elsewhere:

"Do you have other children?" (to each)

"Now let's see—when did you decide to have the next child?"

"Do you remember what you thought the first time you saw your first child? Your second child?" (to each)

"Do you remember what kind of an adult you hoped your child would be?" (to each)

"What kind of plans did you make for the care of the first child when the second child was making his entrance into the world?"

"How did that go?"

"Now, you have two children, a male of three, and an infant girl?"

"What were your observations about how the first child was welcoming the second child?" (to each)

"How had you prepared the first child for the coming of the second child?"

"At this point in time, which one of your children seems most like you?" (to each)

"Which one seems most different from you?" (to each)

"Is there anyone in either of your respective families that any child resembles more than yourself? Who is that person?"

The therapist, by these questions, continually cross-refers information which he has received in order to highlight the realistic concerns which new families have when taking on the parental role. In effect, he lets the parents know that he sees them as having other concerns besides parenting, and as having had to juggle many different kinds of life needs. He also receives clues about how each mate integrated what he expected from the child with what the other mate expected.

53. The therapist tries to get a picture of how much time the members of the family spend together:

"Let's see how a day goes in your house. Who first sees the light of the day?"

"Then who gets up next?"

"Who does that person see when he or she gets up?"

"Then who? Who does that person see? If the other persons in the household already up are gone, where and when did they go?"

The therapist goes on with this until everyone in the household is up, then he takes them through the day to bedtime. Then he makes a statement about the literal clock time that all have for face-to-face contact. He asks about the means everyone has of letting the others know what is going on in his life in the absence of face-to-face contact. If there is no means, then he suggests that each person has a concept of what the others are doing during their absence. He finds out what these concepts are, and checks with the other persons to ascertain the accuracy of the concepts.

54. The therapist will now try to get a picture of the home. He asks who sleeps where? Who eats together? When is eating

done? He tries to get an idea of the atmosphere of the family's life together. He may ask, for example: "If I were in your house during any evening meal or breakfast, what would I see and hear?" (he asks this of each family member, starting with the husband and wife, then going on to the children, oldest first.)

55. The therapist now begins to echo the questions he has asked of the parents by asking some of the same questions of their child (and he accompanies his questions with encouraging and interpretive statements):

> "Do you see your parents as able to have fun? What do you see them doing that is fun?"

> "How do you see your parents as different? (Well, one thing we know for sure: Dad is a male and Mother is a female.)"

> "Do you see your parents as able to disagree openly? How do you see them going about it?"

> "Are you able to relieve their pain? How does Dad respond when you try? How does Mother respond when you try?"

By this stage in the chronology, the therapist has (hopefully) built a safe, understanding framework within which child and mates will be able to comment on what they see and hear. But the therapist is still working against great odds with the child: the child is responding to prohibitions against commenting or even against asking questions.

The therapist continues to accentuate "pain" rather than "who did what to whom?" He now overtly works at releasing the child from parental prohibitions against comments. Also, by asking the child to communicate his perceptions of his parents, the therapist helps the parents receive another view of themselves. Children are very protective of their parents. The more dysfunctional the family, the more protective the children will be. So whatever the children say will be said with great care. Often the parents react by saying, "I never knew that he was aware of all this!"

56. If the child has difficulty commenting, the therapist helps him to do so, and interprets for him:

> "Maybe you are afraid that you will hurt Mother and Dad if you let them know that you see their pain."

> "Maybe you think that if you simply report on what you see and hear, Mother and Dad will only have more pain."

> "I think you *do* see your parents' pain. But maybe you feel you cannot comment."

> "I'm sure Mother and Dad want to know what you see and hear. But maybe they think you don't want to tell them."

57. By this time, the interview is nearing an end. The therapist brings about closure and at the same time stimulates hope:

> "Well, it seems clear that everyone is trying to please everyone else, but no one seems to be successful at this. How can this be! We'll have to work on this!"

> "Once we get all the pieces together so that they make sense this kind of robbery won't have to go on any longer."

> "I have the feeling that we can come to some new ideas about all this."

> "We'll see what else we can learn about all of this. I have the impression that once all of these things get put in their right places, there won't be any more pain."

People do not dare go from the known to the unknown without hope, especially if they are operating within a fearful, critical environment.

58. The family life chronology, as outlined here, looks entirely too neat.

176

a. Interviews are, of course, never this structured or this orderly.

b. Nor does the therapist plow through a chronology regardless of the kind of responses he receives from the family.

c. After all, one of the main purposes of taking a chronology is to shift focus from the Identified Patient to the marital relationship in the least threatening way.

d. If the mates are so fearful that they resist such a shift, the therapist must change his order and change his emphasis slightly.

59. The chronology listed here is really a general plan from which the therapist deviates, depending on responses he receives to questions.

a. Via this plan, he introduces new concepts into the family's ideology, concepts to which he will return in later sessions.

b. Via this plan, he can move quickly but safely into his role as therapist, find out what he needs to work on first, what can wait.
    — He behaves like a dentist who asks the patient, "Where is the pain?" and then proceeds to look where the patient points and explore further.
    — He relies on the family to help him, but he never forgets that he is the leader of the therapy process.

Main Flow of Family-Life Chronology

TO FAMILY AS A WHOLE:

Therapist asks about the problem

TO MATES:

Asks about how they met, when they decided to marry, etc.

TO WIFE:		**TO HUSBAND:**
Asks how she saw her parents, her sibs, her family life.	←——————→	Asks how he saw his parents, his sibs, his family life.
Brings chronology back to when she met her husband.	←——————→	Brings chronology back to when he met his wife.
Asks about her expectations of marriage.	←——————→	Asks about his expectations of marriage.

TO MATES:

Asks about early married life. Comments on influence of past.

TO MATES AS PARENTS:

Asks about their expectations of parenting. Comments on the influence of the past.

TO CHILD:

Asks about his views of his parents, how he sees them having fun, disagreeing, etc

TO FAMILY AS A WHOLE:

Reassures family that it is safe to comment.

Stresses need for clear communication.

Gives closure, points to next meeting, gives hope.

CHAPTER XIII

Including the Children in Family Therapy

1. Many therapists wonder how to introduce children into family therapy.

   a. Even a therapist who has had practice in seeing marital pairs together in therapy is often apprehensive about bringing children in too. It seems a difficult enough task to work with an unhappy marital pair, let alone with two generations at once.

   b. The presence of children might spell anarchy to the therapy process.
      — Children, especially little ones, have limited attention spans and act impulsively.
      — How can a verbal process like therapy hold their interest?
      — How can a child be expected to sit still for an hour or more?

2. Even though the idea of family therapy seems to make sense to a therapist, he may still wonder what rules he should use.

   a. Should he include all the children who are in the family, even the little ones?

   b.   Or should he limit therapy to the two parents and the child who happens to have symptoms?

   c.   Should he include the children right from the beginning? If not, when should he bring them in?

   d.   Once in, how long should the children stay in?

   e.   Once in, what guidelines should the therapist follow in order to keep control of the therapy process?

   f.   Does the presence of children turn family therapy into child therapy?

3. Let me try to explain how I have answered these questions for myself. I will also give a picture of how I, as therapist, proceed. Let us say that Johnny is the I.P. He has a sister, Patty, and a mother and father called Mary and Joe.

   a.   Johnny, by his behavior, is sending "SOS" signals about family pain.

   b.   As I have said before, I include Johnny in therapy with his parents because I see his symptoms as a family phenomenon to be treated by a family approach.

4. What about the other children in the family, in this case, Patty? If Patty has no symptoms, do I still include her in therapy?

   a.   Some family therapists do not include Patty unless she begins showing symptomatic behavior too.

   b.   I do include Patty because Patty is still part of the family homeostasis even though she is not serving an I.P. function.

   c.   I operate from the assumption that when there is pain in the family, all family members feel it in some way. Patty, too, is affected by the pain between her parents, and though she shows no symptoms now, she may later.

   d. I believe that the family therapist can do a great deal of
       preventive work by including all the children in the
       therapy process.
       — As the therapist works to help the family redefine its
         relationships, Patty can become very involved and
         may benefit as much as her brother does.
       — And, because every family member has his own
         perceptions about what is going on in the family,
         Patty will have as much to contribute to the therapy
         process as her brother.

5. If Johnny and Patty are very young, is it still important to
   include them in therapy? After all, one might say that since
   the problem exists mainly between the marital pair, Patty
   and Johnny will benefit just as much if they stay home
   while their parents go in for some marital therapy. Besides,
   any problem that such children have is probably not
   "internalized" yet, so a change in the family environment
   should produce changes in the children even if they are not
   present at therapy sessions.

   a. It is true that Patty and Johnny will benefit if I see only
       their parents in marital therapy. That is why sometimes
       I do see the marital pair when the children are four or
       younger.

   b. But I still make it a point to bring all the children into
       therapy for at least two sessions so that I can see with
       my own eyes how the family, as a whole, operates.

6. I usually see the marital pair first, for at least two sessions. I
   do this because I consider it appropriate to start off family
   therapy with the marital pair.

   a. By asking to see the parents first, I say, in effect: "I see
       you two as the authorized leaders of this family. I also
       see you, apart from the children, as mates."
       — In dysfunctional families, the mates have usually
         despaired of or abandoned their marital roles and
         have become just parents, focused on their children
         because they dare not focus on one another.
       — By the time such a pair comes to me for help for their
         child, very little of what I call "selfing" and of what I

call "husbanding" and "wifing" is evident in their behavior. "Mothering" and "fathering" predominate in one form or another.

— It seems appropriate, therefore, to begin with marital instead of family therapy, in order to remind the pair that they are individuals as well as mates, mates as well as parents.

b. If a family is so dysfunctional, however, that the mates cannot bear to look at their own relationship but must have the child there to focus on, I find it best not to begin with marital therapy but to include the children right from the start. Though I do not consider it appropriate, it is an exception I sometimes have to make.

c. The age of the child helps to determine whether I include him from the beginning or bring him in later. For instance, I include from the start an I. P. "child" who is over 21.

— Many cases of schizophrenia are of this type.
— Though the parents still regard the I. P. as a child, that in itself is part of the family pathology and I do not want to reinforce it.
— Therapists must always stand for reality. I make a point of seeing this "child" and his parents together right away, because I know that the child's symptoms have a family function.
— I make it clear that I am seeing three adults who are on an equal plane with each other. I, by my behavior, am saying: "I do not see your mother and father as still in charge of you. Your mother, father, and I will not meet privately first to decide what to do about you."

7. How long do children stay in family therapy, once I bring them in?

a. As I noted earlier, where the children are under four, I bring them into therapy for at least two of the initial sessions. Otherwise, I work with the marital pair. Later on, though, I may ask to have the I. P. included again in order to consolidate with the child what the mates have learned from their marital therapy.

b. If the children are four or older, they will stay in family therapy for most of the sessions. However, I usually ask for a few sessions along the way with just the marital partners, or with other groupings or individuals (see pages 165–166):

c. Children who are over 21 are also likely to stay in family therapy for most of the sessions.
   — My aim is, of course, to bring such a "child" and his parents together so that I can eventually help separate them.
   — Unfortunately, it almost always takes many family therapy sessions to achieve this goal.
   — In such a family, the child is never supposed to become an adult.

8. Now let me describe how I proceed as therapist, once children have been included in the therapy process.

a. First of all, during the marital therapy sessions, I try to prepare the parents for bringing the children in.
   — Young parents especially are apt to be apprehensive. They wonder how their children will behave. They wonder what I will think of them as parents.
   — I try to reassure them by commenting that of course seven-year-olds act like seven-year-olds, so why should their children be any different?

b. Often I ask the parents how they plan to tell their children about the coming family therapy sessions.
   — Mary may plan to say, "We are going to see a lady and talk about the family."
   — Joe may plan to say, "We are all going for a ride in the car."
   — This very question about how Mary and Joe communicate plans to their children can prepare the ground for later exploration into how clearly or unclearly they get their messages across in the family.
   — In our marital therapy sessions, I have already introduced the idea that Mary and Joe are not very good at communicating with each other, so they will be prepared when I apply this concept to their parenting.

9. Now the day arrives for the first interview with the whole family. Let us say it is going to be an interview with very young children. How does the therapist control them? How does he keep them from bringing anarchy to the therapy process? I will try to make this point clearer in a minute by describing actual interview situations. For the moment, I will try to generalize my main therapy approach.

   a. I have found that a therapist has very few problems of control if he actively takes charge of the therapy process. If he knows how to do this, children respond as readily as their parents.

   b. There are, of course, some control problems.
      — Patty wants to bang on the radiator. Johnny wants to keep going to the bathroom or the drinking fountain.
      — Both constantly interrupt their parents, the therapist and each other in a mad dash to monopolize the airwaves.

   c. My general policy is, of course, to wait for the parents to do the controlling.
      — The mother and father are the ones who should answer requests and set limits to their children's behavior.
      — As a matter of fact, if I took over this role I would lose the very opportunity I am after, the opportunity to observe how the mother and father perform their parenting function.

   d. I do make it my responsibility, however, to communicate clearly the rules of behavior that apply in my own bailiwick, the therapy room
      — No one may hit or play with the microphone or the recording equipment, for example.
      — No one may destroy any chairs, window blinds, tablecloths, etc.
      — No one (including parents, for that matter) may speak for others.
      — Everyone must speak so he can be heard.
      — Everyone must make it possible for others to be heard. "You are hurting my eardrums," I will say, or "You will have to take turns talking or I can't do my work."
      — The parents will often ask me to set a rule about leaving the therapy room. Mother will ask, "Is it all right if he leaves?" I will say, "Yes," and then instruct

the child on how to find the water fountain or the
toilet.
— I also set rules on how often a child may leave the
therapy room. Usually one trip to the toilet and one
trip to the water fountain will give Johnny or Patty all
the chance they need to explore.
— I also shorten the length of the therapy session to
conform to the ages of the children.

e. But, as I have already suggested, there is very little need
for control if the therapist conveys clearly, right from
the beginning, that he is going some place. The children
can get caught up in the therapy process; they can
become as engrossed in it as their parents.

10. For instance, there are certain things I want to do from the
beginning of family therapy. I want to use the opening
sessions for diagnosis, but I also want to use them for
therapy. Therefore, I try right away to introduce certain
concepts that are usually foreign to the dysfunctional family.
These concepts are probably familiar to you by now, but I
think they can bear repeating. I want the family members:

a. To recognize that they are individuals and are different
from one another.
— Some are males, some are females. Some have red
hair, some brown. Some like roast beef, some hate it.
Some are young, some older.
— Dysfunctional families have great trouble
acknowledging different-ness or individuality. In such
families, to be different is to be bad and invites being
unloved.

b. To recognize that they also have disagreements.
— Some see a certain picture as beautiful, others see it
as ugly. Some think a certain piece of behavior is
desirable, others see it as undesirable.
— Dysfunctional families often try to overlook or to
"blur" their disagreements, whether these are
disagreements over perception or over opinion.

c. To communicate with one another more clearly; to say
what they see, think, feel; to bring disagreements out
into the open.

— I especially want mates to see where they have been
giving conflicting messages to their children as well
as to each other. Marital communication sets the
standard for parental communication and for all
communication between family members.
— I also want children and parents to be able to
recognize and comment on the pain existing between
the marital partners.
— I also want to help family members to communicate
about the behavior which brings them pleasure. As I
have said, dysfunctional families have just as much
trouble communicating about pleasure as they have
communicating about pain.

11. Here is a rather skeletal picture of a first interview with
children present, pointing up the main emphases.

   a. To cover the points listed might take one interview with
   highly verbal young children, or it might take two or
   more.

   b. If even this summary seems long in reading, that is
   because it is described in slow motion here.

   c. However long it takes me to achieve my first therapy
   aims, I ask my questions in a warm, specific,
   matter-of-fact way.
   — I ask many questions, believing that questions are in
   themselves therapeutic. This may be the first time
   that the children have been treated as people with
   perceptions and opinions.
   — And, while I mostly concentrate on the children in the
   first family interview, I am indirectly speaking to the
   parents, too.

12. How the therapist can integrate children into family
therapy:

   a. The therapist introduces the idea of individuality.
   — He greets each child separately, calling him by name.
   — He differentiates each child according to birth order
   and sex:

"Let's see now. You are John. You are the eldest in the family."
— He repeats what each child says, to show that he is listening to the child:

Th: How old are you, Patty?

D: Seven.

Th: You are seven.
— He asks questions over and over (especially with younger children) to say: "I am really talking to you." Often children will say they don't know or don't remember or give no answer at all. But they will give the therapist clues to their answer in what they do. He does not leave an unanswered question without some closure. He says:

"I see you are not ready to tell yet. We will come back to you later. I noticed you were looking at Mother and had a frown on your face. Maybe you are worried about what Mother will say."
— He honors all questions from children to show that questions are not troublemaking and illegitimate, that people can ask questions about what they don't know.

D: (whispering to Johnny) How old is Daddy?

M: And I told him he could play outside if . . .

Th: Excuse me just a minute. Patty had a question here, I think. You were wondering how old Dad is? Well Dad can tell you. It's all right to ask. If Dad doesn't want to tell you he can say so. How about it, Dad? Do you want Patty to know?
— He assumes that children do hear, are interested, and are able to understand. They are not little-and-therefore-bad. He verbalizes his expectations so that children will rise to meet them.

M: He isn't listening. He's always like that.

Th: I'm not so sure. This fellow has his head screwed on right. He knows what's going on. But let's check with him.

b. The therapist introduces the idea of communication:
— He asks each child (according to birth order) what
ideas he has about why he is here. (Little children
feel pushed around.)

> Th: (to Johnny) What ideas did you have about
> where you were going today?

> S: I don't know.

> Th: Well you must have had some ideas about it.
> What did Mother tell you? What did Dad say?
> You must have figured out something to yourself.

— He repeats what each child says (with clarifying
interpretation) and goes on to the next child. (But not
until he has some kind of answer from each child.)

> Th: (to Patty) You thought you were going to talk?
> What did you think you were going to talk about?

> D: Oh, the family.

> Th: You got the idea that we were going to talk about
> the family. And Johnny, what ideas did you
> have?

— He summarizes answers received from the children in
terms of how clear they seemed to be about why they
are in the therapy room:

> "So Johnny thought he was going for a ride. Patty
> thought she was going to talk about the family. So
> you both had ideas about it."

— He asks each child where he got his ideas about why
he is here. Who told him? What was said?

> D: Mother said we were going to talk about family
> problems.

> Th: What about Dad? Did he tell you the same thing?

> D: No.

> Th: What did Dad say?

> D: He said we were going for a ride.

Th: I see. So you got some information from Mother and some information from Dad. What about you, Johnny? Where did you get your information?

S: I don't remember.

Th: You don't remember who told you?

M: I don't think I said anything to him, come to think of it. He wasn't around at the time, I guess.

Th: How about you, Dad? Did you say anything to Johnny?

F: No, I thought Mary had told him.

Th: (to Johnny) Well, then, how *could* you remember if nothing was said?

S: Patty said we were going to see a lady about the family.

Th: I see. So you got your information from your sister, whereas Patty got a clear message from both Mother and Dad.

— He asks how they handled differences in messages from their parents:

S: Daddy told Patty we were going for a ride.

Th: And Mother told Patty you were going to talk to a lady about the family?

S: Yeh.

Th: So what did you do with that? Dad is saying one thing and Mother another? You have to figure that one out. What did you make of that?

S: I figured we would go for a ride. And, uh, we would see a lady or something . . .

Th: I see. You decided that you would be doing both. So in this case, you were able to fit these things together—what Mother and Dad said to Patty.

S: Uh huh.

— He asks the mother and father what they remember saying:

> Th: How about that, Mother? Were you and Dad able to work this out together—what you would tell the children?

> M: Well, you know, I think this is one of our problems. He does one thing with them and I do another.

> F: I think this is a pretty unimportant thing to worry about.

> Th: Of course it is, in one sense. But then we can use it, you know, to see how messages get across in the family.

— He makes a general statement about communication:

> "One of the things we work on in families is how family members communicate—how clearly they get their messages across. We will have to see how Mother and Dad can get together so that Johnny and Patty can get a clear message."

c. The therapist briefly introduces the idea that family members can acknowledge parents' pain.

— He explains to the children why their mother and father have been coming here:

> "Well, now, I'll tell you why Mother and Dad have come here. They have come here because they were unhappy about how things were going in the family and they want to work out ways so that everyone can get more pleasure from family life."

— He asks each child if he noticed that his mother and father were unhappy and asks for the evidence he uses for this perception:

> Th: Had you noticed that Mother and Dad weren't happy, Patty?

> D: Yes, a little bit.

Th: Well, I would think you could see when Mother and Dad had pain. What have you noticed about this?

D: Mother cries sometimes.

Th: Mother cries sometimes. And, of course, tears mean that Mother is feeling pain.

D: Mother doesn't cry very often, though.

Th: Of course Mother has her happy times, too. How about Dad. Have you noticed when Dad has pain?

— He summarizes what each child has said and leaves the topic for the moment:

> "So Patty knows crystal-clearly when Mother has pain but she isn't quite as sure about Dad. Johnny says he hasn't noticed any pain except when Dad gets mad at him. We will find out more about that later."

d. The therapist returns to the idea that family members can acknowledge different-ness, especially sex differentness, while at the same time he continues to establish rapport with each child.
— He asks each child in more detail about himself:

Th: All right, we know Johnny is the eldest. He is also the only boy. What grade are you in, Johnny?

S: Sixth.

Th: What do you like about school?

S: Baseball. I'm on first base.

Th: So we have a baseball player in the family. How about Dad, does he play baseball too?

S: Oh he's all right . . .

F: I used to play a little.

Th: So you both have this in common. What else do
you like about school?
— He makes general comments to each child about age
problems each would be likely to have in relation to
the other sib:

"Does this one get in your hair sometimes?"

"Does that one kind of push you around
sometimes?"

"I would expect ten-year-old boys not to want little
girls around."
— He highlights the sex balance in the family:

"Then this is a family which has two females in it
and two males in it. So nobody can be outnumbered
in this family!"

"So you and Dad kind of hold up the male end of
the household."
— He asks each parent to describe each child in order to
help them acknowledge different-ness:

M: Well, she is much quieter than he is. She tends
to be more serious.

Th: You see Patty as the quiet one and the serious
one. How about you, Dad? Is that what you see as
different about the two?

F: Yes, she is more like her mother. Johnny isn't
really like anyone in the family.

Th: Johnny seems so different that he doens't seem
like a member of the family?

F: Most of the time, the way he behaves, yes.
— He helps children acknowledge ordinary different-ness
between their parents:

Th: How do you see your mother and your father as
different, Johnny?

S: I don't know.

> Th: Well, they have to be different, you know. No two people are alike. One thing we know for sure, Dad is a male, Mother is a female. That's a big difference.

e. The therapist introduces the idea that parents can have differences of opinion and disagreements, and can feel anger toward their children.
— He asks each child how he knows when Dad is angry:

> Th: (to Johnny) How does Dad go about showing his anger?

> S: He just gets mad.

> Th: Of course he does. Everybody gets mad sometimes. I would hope that Dad would have ways to let you know when he is not pleased with something you do. How does he show that he is mad?

— He asks the same question about Mother:

> Th: How do you know, Patty, when Mother is angry with you?

> D: Oh, I know.

> Th: Then Mother is able to let you know this clearly?

> D: She spanks me.

> Th: She spanks you. Can you tell ahead of time when Mother will spank you?

> D: When I do something bad.

> Th: Like what?

> D: If I break my doll. If I go into the street . . .

— He compares the two parents' ways of showing anger:

> "Oh, so Dad shuts up and won't talk to you? You know something is going on but maybe you aren't sure what. Mother tells you right out what she

doesn't like. Are you sure what Dad is angry about? You seem to know what displeases Mother."
— He asks what things make each parent angry:

Th: What do you know, as sure as tomorrow is Wednesday, will make Dad blow his cork?

S: If I play with his tools.

Th: If you play with his tools. What else?
— He asks how each child decides what to do if his parents don't agree on what should be done:

Th: Mother says you must play in your room. Dad tells you to play outside. Those are two different things. How do you know what to do?

S: Uh . . . I . . . uh.

Th: How *can* you know what to do?

M: He plays both ends against the middle. That's what he does.

Th: Well, of course he would have a problem here. Maybe if he does what Dad wants, then it looks as if he doesn't love Mother. He would have a problem here as to what he should do.

f. The therapist introduces the idea that parents can have differences of opinion and can feel anger toward each other.
— He asks each child how his parents go about disagreeing:

Th: Of course everybody disagrees every once in a while. Let's see now, if I were in your house and Mother and Dad were mad at each other, what would I see?

S: Mother goes to her room.

D: Mother cries.

Th: Mother would be in her room crying. And where would Dad be?

S: Daddy usually beats it.

Th: Dad tries to solve things by leaving the house?

D: Daddy gets mad when Mother cries.

Th: How do you decide this? That Dad is mad because Mother cries?

D: He slams the door.

Th: I see. Dad slams the door. Mother is crying in her room. What do you see happening, Johnny?

— He asks each mate to say how he or she knows when the other is angry or displeased:

Th: How about that, Dad? Do tears make you angry? Or are you already mad at Mary for something and then Mary cries?

F: Somehow . . . I don't know . . . somehow she has this way of letting me feel that it's me . . . that I am the one who . . .

Th: Mary's tears make you feel you've been the one who is wrong, is that it? You feel at fault?

F: Exactly. She won't listen when I try to explain.

Th: What about you, Mary? How do you know when Joe is displeased?

M: He turns on the TV so loud you can hear it in the laundry room.

Th: So then he shows his anger by shutting you out, is that it? And she shows her anger by shutting you out with her tears. And either way you can't find a way to get close enough to work things out.

— He asks each mate what he does when other mate is angry, and how he tries to solve the disagreement:

F: I give in. That's what I do.

M: That's what you think. You're as stubborn as they come.

F: How? How am I more stubborn than you?

M: *Many's* the time I've come around to you.

Th: I think that . . .

S: Daddy, when are we going to the beach? You promised we could go, and we never do.

F: As soon as it's warmer we'll go. It's too cold to go to the beach.

M: Of course we did promise them . . .

Th: I think we should . . .

D: You said we could go a couple of weeks ago.

Th: I think both children get upset when their mother and father disagree. Maybe they think someone will get hurt. But I don't see any dead bodies around, do you? Mother looks in one piece. Dad looks in one piece.

M: They do get upset. We try not to argue in front of the kids.

Th: But of course they know when their parents have pain. The important thing is that ways can be found to work on this. That's why we are here, to find ways to work on this.

g. The therapist ends the first interview by introducing the idea that each family member must show it when he is pleased by what any of the others do.
— He asks each child what he can do that makes his mother or his father pleased.
— He asks each parent what he or she can do that pleases each child.
— He asks each mate what he can do that pleases the other mate.
— He comments on the information received:

"Well, then, it seems everyone is clear on how to get everyone else's goat, but they are not clear on how to please each other. This is terrible. We'll have to work on this!"

13. So much for a skeletal picture of the first family interview with young children. Now let us drop in at different times in later family interviews to see what is going on. What is the family therapist now doing? What is the family doing?

   a. The therapist is still working to untangle the dysfunctional relationships which exist in unhappy families and which come about primarily because the marital relationship is askew.
     — Parents are abdicating from parenting.
     — Parents are acting as sibs with their children, vying for attention from the other mate.
     — Children are "parenting" their parents.
     — Children are acting as ersatz mates of their parents.
     — Children are successfully challenging appropriate parental authority.

   b. Whatever family members are doing, the family homeostasis is precarious and all family members are feeling disappointed and puzzled.
     — Nothing seems to turn out right.
     — There never seems to be enough of anything to go around.
     — Any relationship between any two members in the family makes the others feel left out.
     — Evil motives are attributed to everyone.
     — Everyone is feeling cheated.

   c. Yet in spite of these conditions, the family as a whole still resists the efforts of any family member to change the family's way of operating. It takes a lot of therapist intervention to bring any pleasure to the family's life.

14. How the therapist can make parental behavior and child behavior understandable to family members.

   a. The therapist helps parents to understand their children and receive "feedback" from them.
     — He asks the parents to explain the child's behavior, thus making covert explanations overt so they can be

dealt with. He challenges any solely negative interpretations and answers covert questions parents are asking about their children.

M: His pleasure is doing things he knows will get me up in the air. Every minute he's in the house . . . constantly.

Th: There's no pleasure to that, my dear.

M: Well, there is to him.

Th: No. You can't see his thoughts. You can't get inside his skin. All you can talk about is what you see and hear. You can say it *looks* as though it's for pleasure.

M: All right. Well, it looks as though, and that's just what it looks like constantly.

Th: He could be trying to keep your attention, you know. It is very important to Johnny what Mother thinks.

— He asks the child to explain his own behavior:

F: I mean, he never wanted me to stay and watch him play baseball.

Th: Tell me, how did you explain this to yourself? Why did you think he didn't want you to watch?

F: Well, that's the trouble, I never have been able to figure it out.

Th: Well, one way to find out is to *ask.* Let's ask Johnny. He can tell you. Maybe he is uneasy when Dad is around.

S: I'd just get embarrassed, sometimes.

Th: You'd get embarrassed.

S: Uh huh. Cause he had Patty with him and Patty is always making a fuss. The other guys would laugh . . .

— He helps the child to express frustration and anger
and delineate situations which precipitate anger:

> Th: Do you kind of get made at Daddy when he gets
> mad at you?

> S: Yeah, and sometimes he gets real mad and
> pinches my ear.

> Th: He pinches your ear. Do you feel like hitting him
> back?

> S: Yeah. I get real mad sometimes.

> Th: So what keeps you from hitting him?

> S: Well he's, uh, he's bigger than me.

b. The therapist helps children to understand their parents
and to understand themselves as children.
— He asks children to explain a parent's behavior, in
order to challenge solely negative interpretations and
add other possible interpretations:

> Th: Johnny, why do you think your mother wants
> you to eat?

> S: I don't know. She's always forcing things on me
> to eat.

> Th: You know what? Let me tell you something about
> mothers. Mothers rack their brains trying to
> figure out what will please the family. Then, at
> the table, when you turn up your nose and say
> "That! I won't eat it!" what's mother to do? You
> are saying to her, "Take your food and stick it. I
> don't like it." Well, then mother feels, "What can
> I do? I don't know how to please you. OK, I won't
> try anymore. I can't please you, so I might as
> well not try."

— He asks parents to explain their own behavior toward
children:

> Th: Tell me, why don't you want him to eat sweets?

M: I don't mind if he eats sweets, but he can't live on a constant diet of sweets.

Th: Well, why not? I thought everybody lived on a constant diet of sweets. Isn't that sensible?

M: No, and especially at that age. Your face breaks out and everything else.

Th: Why don't you let him be pimply? What do you care? What do you care like that for?

M: Well, I don't know . . .

Th: Well, see, I think . . .

M: All he does . . . he sleeps at our house and eats when he pleases, and that's about it.

Th: Do you hear in your mother's voice the irritation that she has when she's talking?

S: Yeah.

Th: Do you also have the feeling that this is a kind of desperation? She's thinking, "How am I going to get this guy grown up? He's going to grow up toothless and pimply and weak, and I can't do anything about it" (parents laugh)

— He helps the child to express openly, and the parents to answer, covert questions the child is asking:

Th: (to Johnny) You're not really sure yet why Dad adopted you, are you?

S: Uuuh.

Th: What?

S: I haven't been thinking about it.

Th: I think you should, because I think part of what you're thinking is that he only did it because your mother made him do it.

S: She can't make him do anything.

Th: Of course not! But then, you know, why did he do it then?

S: I don't know.

Th: Well, you've got to find some explanation, because your dad's a pretty sensible guy and he doesn't go around . . .

S: He must know why he did it.

Th: He must know?

S: Yes.

Th: Well, let's ask him. (pause) Sure he knows why he did it, but I wonder if you know.

S: I don't.

Th: (to father) Tell him again. Why did you adopt this bloke over here?

c. The therapist supports parental authority, at the same time recognizing that children are increasingly able to make good judgements and decisions for themselves.
    — He assumes that parents have the right and responsibility to "parent" their children:

    "You are the mother. You know what bedtime is best for seven-year-olds."
    — He assumes that children can take responsibility for what they do:

    Th: It was clear to you about when you were to be home, Johnny. What kept you from being home at that time?

    *   *   *   *   *   *   *

D: I didn't *mean* to kick him.

Th: Well, let's see now, Patty. It was your leg that somehow landed against his leg. How can a leg do that all by itself? That's very curious.

— He checks our family rules:

Th: What is the rule in this family about watching television.

M: They can watch certain programs each night, up to about nine.

Th: So you have definite rules about that?

M: Oh yes.

Th: What are some of the rules? Johnny, you tell me what rules you know about.

M: Don't eat in the dining room. Don't leave clothes around. Don't let the dog in the house

Th: These rules are very clear to you then? What was the one about not eating in the dining room? That sounds sort of strange to me.

M: Well, you see, we eat in the kitchen usually . . .

F: We use the dining room for guests.

Th: I see. So this family has a very special room for when visitors come in.

— He checks out family rule reinforcement:

Th: How does it go in the family, with discipline?

F: Oh, I don't know, I, ah . . .

M: We try to carry through when we make a promise.

F: Uh . . .

Th: Both ways?

F: Uh huh.

M: Good or bad.

F: Good or bad. Yes.

Th: Do you find yourself a little reluctant on that once in a while?

M: No.

F: I, ah, try to keep it up, ah, if I tell him that he's not going to watch television . . . Of course, he does, he just, ah, that's another one. I told him for two weeks he can't watch television; first thing he's out there watching television.

d. He shows how marital disagreements produce difficulties in parenting (see example on pages 43–44).

e. The therapist helps mates restructure family relationships around a well-delineated marital relationship.
— He helps parents separate themselves from their own parents:

Th: Were you the kind of a gal that could say to your mother: "Now Mama, I'm grown up now. No more of this"?

M: No, no, I won't talk back to my mother.

Th: Is that talking back, or is that stating a simple fact?

M: No, I couldn't conceive of it. Mother would get very mad.

Th: I think this has been a problem in this family.

F: Yes. Too much of one.
— He helps mates to strengthen the marital relationship:

Th: What would you like to do?

M: Aaah, spend more time with him. I, I'm satisfied when he comes home; we don't have to particularly talk . . . I just like to be with him.

F: We like to camp.

M: And we like to camp.

Th: It's kind of natural, you know.

M: Yah! (sharp laugh)

Th: But you say it in a way that says you feel sad about it not happening more often.

M: I do! (long silence)

Th: Well, maybe that is an area where everyone can grow a little bit so that you can have more opportunity.

— He helps equalize the parental responsibilities:

Th: Do you find it's easier to get your messages across to the kids when you and Dad are both home?

M: Yes.

Th: Have you any idea why that might be so?

M: Well, mmm, I don't know. Maybe he figures that Daddy's going to see that it stops—whatever is happening . . .

Th: Does it cross your mind that it must be awfully tough for a woman to take the total responsibility for a family? Any woman would very much feel the loss of a husband during the week.

— He helps strengthen same-sex parent-child relationships:

Th: (to Johnny) You mean you're making some shelves?

S: Yeh.

Th: You're making them with Dad?

S: No, I was watching one day. And we do a lot of Scout work together, and we made this little mail box.

Th: Good for you and Dad, that you have these times together.
— He indirectly encourages same-sex parent-child relationships by questioning overdeveloped opposite-sex relationships:

Th: So you mean it's known in the family that you and Patty have always been quite close?

F: Real close, very close.

Th: (to mother) What about your son? Does he have the same kind of relationship to you?

F· Yes, oh yes.

M: (faintly) Yes, that's right.

Th: Is that how it is? A mother and son and daddy and daughter kind of thing?
— He helps mates attend to each other more and to the children less:

Th: You know, both of you are turning yourselves inside out so much for your kids you have no time for yourselves.

M: I don't think we do more than parents should do.

Th: Well, tell me something. What are the two of you likely to do together?

S: I just had poison oak.

Th: What's that?

S: I just had poison oak a little while ago.

F: One of the hazards of camping.

M: Yes indeed.

S: I just had it the last time camping.

M: He lost two days of school that last week.

Th: And you went camping all that time?

S: Uh huh.

Th: What are you two likely to do if you just go off for a holiday or when you have time together?

M: He and I?

Th: Just you and George, yes.

M: We don't go off by ourselves as a rule.

F: We did once I think, aah, you know the last time we went down South we went to . . .

M: Oh, well, well, we had to, aaah . . .

F: We went to a funeral.

15. Theoretically, seeing families together in therapy makes good sense to most therapists, but they still feel apprehensive as to how to go about it. I hope this necessarily sketchy and incomplete description will give some idea of how it can be done.

    a. One fact we cannot overlook is that family therapy seems to make sense to the family itself.

    b. Husbands, in particular, participate readily in this kind of therapy.

    c. Both husband and wife repeatedly say, "We should have done this a long time ago."

CHAPTER XIV

Role and Technique of the Therapist

1. The therapist must first create a setting in which people can, perhaps for the first time, take the risk of looking clearly and objectively at themselves and their actions.

   a. He must concentrate on giving them confidence, reducing their fears, and making them comfortable and hopeful about the therapy process.

   b. He must show that he has direction, that he is going somewhere. His patients come to him because he is an expert, so he must accept the label and be comfortable in his role.

   c. Above all, he must show patients that he can structure his questions in order to find out what both he and they need to know.

2. The patient is afraid. He doesn't dare ask about what he doesn't know; he feels little, alone and frightened.

   a. He suffers from the Crystal Ball Syndrome: "I'm supposed to know. But I am little and can't ask. Yet I am big and omniscient; I can guess. You, the therapist, should be able to guess too."

b. He suffers from the Fragility Syndrome: "If I ask, the other person will fall apart. If I ask, I will get an answer that will make *me* fall apart."

c. He suffers from Fear of the Unknown. Pieces of the past are missing or can't be looked at. This or that is forbidden territory.

d. He doesn't know what it is he doesn't know; he feels hopeless. He has been operating from insufficient information for a long time. He feels that there is no point in continuing the struggle.

e. He can't ask about what he doesn't know; he feels helpless. Sick people can't be direct about what they want. They can tell about what hurts, not about what is wrong.

f. He fears the therapist will lie to him; he feels suspicious. He assumes that others know and won't tell; that others see and hear everything. ("Ma always knew when I was in the cookie jar. So others know what is inside of me.")

3. The therapist is not afraid.

a. He does dare to ask questions, and the way he frames them helps the patient to be less afraid as well.
   — The therapist asks what the patient can answer, so that the patient feels competent and productive.
   — The therapist engages the patient in a history-taking procedure to bring out details of family life. This makes the patient feel he knows things the therapist doesn't know, that he has something to contribute. (Patients get very involved in building this factual history of their own past. They argue with each other about the facts, correct the therapist, and so forth.)
   — The therapist asks questions which the patient can emotionally handle at the time, so the patient can feel he is in control.

b. The therapist doesn't know what it is he doesn't know, but he knows how to find out and how to check on his knowledge.
   — The therapist does not assume anything. He must not think he knows more than he does. All he can assume

is that there is a body before him; it is breathing; it is
a male or a female of a certain age.
— If the therapist operates from assumptions without
checking on them, he is often wrong. He must
question his patients constantly:

> "Does she like being beaten, or not?"

> "Did they ever get to the movies?"

> "What does 'Well, sort of' mean?"

— He must question his own assumptions too. Does their
coming late to the appointment mean they are
"resisting" or not? (There is a story about a man
accused by the therapist of "resisting" therapy
because he arrived late for the therapy hour. Later the
therapist discovered the man had been held up by a
serious accident on the freeway.)

c. The therapist can ask about what he doesn't know; he
knows how to get facts.
— Facts about planning processes: "Did you get to the
movies as you planned?" or, "Did you ever get the
bread on the table?"
— Facts which reveal loopholes in planning. For
instance, the mother complains that her children
don't do chores. The therapist finds by questioning
that she never tells them what to do; all the
instructions are in her head.
— Facts about perceptions of self and other: "How did
you expect he would react?" or, "What did you assume
she thought?"
— Facts about perceptions of roles and models: "Who
does what in your house?" or, "How did your dad
handle money?"
— Facts about communicatioon techniques:

> "You weren't sure what he meant? What was it
> about his behavior that made you uncertain?"

> "What did you say to him? What did you say back
> to her?"

> "Did the words coming out of his mouth match the
> look on his face?"

"Did you try to get your point across? How? Then what did you do?"

— Facts about how members express sexual feelings and act out. The therapist doesn't give double-level messages to patients to the effect that he really wants to hear about these subjects more than any other. His questions concern everyday living, *including* sex activities and periods of acting out. When discussing sexual material, the therapist does so in an open, concrete, matter-of-fact way. He treats this subject like any other. He says: "What way is it?" not, "Who is to blame?"; "How does that go?" not, "Why don't you respond?"

d. The therapist does not fear the patient is lying to him; he is not suspicious. He realizes the patient is not deliberately withholding information or misrepresenting it. He is responding to a vague fear of blame and low self-worth.

4. The therapist shows the patient how he looks to others.

a. The therapist rises above the cultural prohibition against telling others how they manifest themselves:

"Your nose is bleeding."

"Your slip is showing."

"You seem to want to be friends with him, but you don't act the way you say you feel."

"You seem to want to succeed but you act as though you might be afraid to try."

b. The therapist realizes that people are grateful to be told how they manifest themselves.

"We all need three-way mirrors. Yet we assume that others see in us what we feel we are manifesting."

"We can give information if we do it in such a tone that our good will is clear. Clarity of intent gets across if our words, face, tone of voice, are all of a piece."

But such information must also be given in an appropriate context, in an appropriate relationship. The telling must not be overdone, and good things must be told too. For example, a husband had a glob of something on his shoe. He and his wife sat through a whole therapy session with me. Finally the wife mentioned it to her husband. He asked her why she hadn't told him, and she said she didn't want to embarrass him or hurt him. Also, she thought he knew about it. He was angry that she hadn't told him. Even though the news we get from others may be uncomfortable, we prefer that to not knowing the impression we give.

c. The therapist can also put the tape recorder to good use. Playing back tapes of previous conversations (which were openly recorded, of course) can be a good way of showing people how they sound and look to others, as well as making it easier for patient and therapist to study the interactions of therapy. In addition, the positive moves of patients can be pointed out to them while playing back tapes.

5. When the therapist asks for and gives information, he does so in a matter-of-fact, nonjudgmental, light, congruent way.

   a. The therapist verbally recreates situations in order to collect facts. He has a flair for acceptance and imagination:

      Th: Now let me see. There was no bread. What did you do for bread that night?

      W: Well, we didn't have any.

      Th: Well, then you didn't get enough to eat. Now let's take a look at what you were trying to do. You wanted food on the table and it wasn't there. And you thought Harry was going to bring it. Your husband is telling you that you don't keep him informed, and you are telling him he doesn't care what happens in the house, what happens to you. Let's see where this all started. Here you are, Harry, coming in the door wondering if dinner's cooked. And your wife is thinking, "We don't have any bread . . ."

b. By showing he is easy about giving and receiving information, the therapist makes it easier for the patient to do so.
— I can ask—so can you.
— I can give information—so can you.
— I can receive information—so can you.
— I can give a clear message—so can you.

(But the therapist must beware of the inappropriate light touch. One time a trainee-therapist sat with a smile on her face while a patient was telling her about very painful material. The trainee's consultant-observer pointed this out to her after the session was over. She was unaware that she was doing this, and said she guessed she always smiled when things were painful to cover up what she was feeling inside. The therapist must be congruent in his behavior.)

6. The therapist builds self-esteem.

a. The therapist makes constant "I value you" comments along the way:

"You're a responsible person."

"You have feelings too, you know."

"You can want things for yourself, can't you?"

b. The therapist labels assets. The patient is like a grocery store after an earthquake, with unlabeled goods lying all around. The therapist takes a tally for the patient; what is in stock, how it might be sold. The therapist says:

"You showed you could do that quite well."

"You never allowed yourself to develop that, did you?"

c. The therapist asks the patient questions he can answer (see page 159).

d. The therapist emphasizes that he and his patients are equals in learning.
  — By asking questions, he tells his patients: "You contribute to what I know." (Family members check each other on facts and this should be encouraged.)
  — He admits that he can make mistakes: "I goofed on that. I'm sorry," or, "I forgot. It was careless of me. I should have remembered."
  — By his actions, he tells his patients, "I share what I know." The therapist shares as much of his assumptions and knowledge as he can, but at the right time and in an appropriate manner.

e. The therapist includes himself as a person whose meaning can be checked on: "I will try to be perfectly clear. You check me if you don't follow me."

f. The therapist takes the family's history and notes past achievements.

g. The therapist begins to accentuate the idea of good intentions but bad communication:

> "I think Mother and Dad very much want to get across their messages, but somehow something seems to stand in their way."

> "In this family I see everyone wanting to report on what they see and hear and on what they wish for, but somehow behaving as though others won't hear."

> "There is no lack of good intentions, good wishes in this family. But somehow everyone seems to have trouble making these wishes clear."

> "I don't think for a minute that anyone in this family wants to give pain to others. But when comments are made, they always seem to come out in the form of accusations."

"Why is it that members of this family don't seem able to give open reports to each other on what they see and hear?"

h. The therapist asks each family member what he can do that brings pleasure to another member:

> "What can you do, Joe, that you know ahead of time will bring pleasure to Mary?" (and vice versa)

> "What can you do, Johnny, that will bring big smiles to Mother's face?"

By these questions the therapist not only further delineates family rules, but he helps each member to see himself as others see him. Maybe Johnny says (about his father): "I can't do anything to please him." Maybe Joe says (about what he thinks his wife wants of him): "Just bring in the money." Maybe Mary says (about what Joe wants of her): "Just keep him fed."

i. The therapist is human, clear, direct. Love is not enough. The therapist works for maximum adaptability by helping the family to feel they are likeable. He raises their capacity to give and minimizes their sensitivities to painful subjects, thereby decreasing the necessity for defenses.

7. The therapist decreases threat by setting the rules of interaction.

a. The therapist sees to it that all are present: "We need your reaction, experience, on this," or, "Only you can tell us what you saw and heard."

b. He makes it clear that no one is to interrupt others:

> "You're all talking at once. I can't hear."

> "I guess Johnny will have to speak for five minutes, then Patty can speak for five minutes."

> "You're hurting my eardrums."

c. He emphasizes that no one may act out or make it impossible to converse during the session:

> "I have to hear in order to do my work."

> "You got your point across. Now let's get to work."

> "No wonder you have not been able to work this out. Nobody is listening to anybody else."

> "Now I know how deeply you feel about this. There's no further need to show me."

> "When you can talk in an adult manner, then come back and we'll get to work. Until then we will have to terminate therapy."

d. He makes sure that no one is allowed to speak for anybody else:

> "When you speak, speak for yourself only."

> "Let Johnny speak for himself. You can't be an authority on Johnny."

> "Have you ever crawled inside another's head and looked at a thought? You can't do it. Neither can I. We have to check."

> "You can collect evidence on his behavior and on what he says and see if they fit. You can then ask about it. But only he can explain why his messages didn't fit."

> "Did you ever *ask* what he meant by what he said? Or did you just guess?"

e. He tries to make everyone speak out clearly so he can be heard.

f. He makes direct requests to people to speak up:

> "I'm a little deaf. Not very deaf, but a little deaf. You're going to have to speak up."

"We don't want to miss what you have to say."

"Maybe you feel that what you have to say isn't important."

g. He kids:

"Cat get your tongue?"

"Know the language?"

"You need practice in exercising that lower lip."

h. He relates silence to covert controls:

"I saw you looking at Mother. Were you thinking she didn't want you to speak?"

"Maybe you think if you speak you'll get clobbered."

"We'll have to find out what makes it so unsafe to talk."

8. The therapist decreases threat by the way he structures the interviews:

a. The therapist announces that therapy is aiming toward a concrete goal and will have a definite end.
— At the very beginning he sets boundaries: "This is not going to be an open-ended process, one which may drag on indefinitely. The total number of interviews within which we shall try to work will be . . ."
— He may also set more limited deadlines: "At the end of five sessions, we shall re-evaluate to see what has been accomplished, where we need to go."

b. The therapist plans the interviews so that the family will understand that he sees them as a *family* and is not taking anyone's side.
— He may begin therapy by seeing the two mates, the "architects" of the family, or he may see the whole family together. But whenever he starts with a new family, he wants to see them all together at least once, even when the children are too young to enter

therapy, in order to understand the operation of the family and what each person's place in it is.

— He never sees the I. P. and his parents alone, as this would only reinforce the common assumption that the I. P. is the root of the family's trouble.

— He never sees any unit other than the parents alone before he and the family are clear on the whole family's way of operating. Doing so before this understanding is reached may make the therapist appear to be in a coalition with certain family members, or getting privileged data which may be kept from other members. The therapist must guard against any actions which might be taken by the family as a message about "who is to blame," "who is loved most," "who is sick," etc.

— After the operation of the family is made explicit to the therapist and the family, he can see individuals on a basis understood by everyone to pertain to some work relating to a marital pair, an individual, the sibling unit, and so forth.

— The therapist singles out units when it seems practical or feasible. Sometimes family members are away for business or camp and seeing the separated units comes about naturally. If he sees anyone separately, it is always with the idea of reporting back to the family group what he and they have "discovered."

9. The therapist decreases threat by reducing the need for defenses.

a. In my opinion, the dysfunctional family operates within a reign of terror, with all members fearing they will be hurt and all members fearing they will hurt others. All comments are taken as attacks on self-esteem. Therefore, the therapist must reduce terror. Defenses, as I see them, are simply ways of enhancing self-esteem and defending against attacks on self-esteem. So the therapist does not have to "destroy" defenses in order to produce change. He exerts all his efforts to reducing terror, reducing the necessity for defenses.

b. The therapist asks each family member what he can do that brings anger from another member:

"What can you do which you know, as sure as sure, will make Dad blow his cork?"

"What can you do, Mary, that will make Joe especially mad?"

Such questions further delineate family rules and prohibitions. They help family members make covert rules overt. They also continue to decrease fears about showing anger.

c. The therapist interprets anger as hurt:

> "Well, as far as I am concerned, when a person looks angry, this simply means he feels pain inside. In some way he feels his self-esteem is in danger."

> "We will have to work out ways so that you can all give clear messages without feeling you will hurt other people's feelings."

> "Dad may look angry but he is really feeling some kind of pain and hurt. He will have to give a clearer message about his pain, so that others will know what is going on inside him."

d. The therapist acknowledges anger as a defense and deals with the hurt:

> H: It's all I can do to keep from killing you!

> W: You're a mean old man!

> Th: Now I know how deeply disappointed you both are. Things have turned out so differently from what you hoped. Let's see what happened which has prevented the two of you from having joy and pleasure in your lives.

e. The therapist shows that pain and the forbidden are all right to look at:

> "Did you see your parents' pain? Were you able to relieve it?"

"So your dad had a wooden leg. You couldn't talk about that, could you? That was painful for your family to talk about. Why?"

"So Roger was adopted. Did you know this, Roger? What did Mother tell you about it? Why weren't you able, Mother, to tell Roger this?"

f.   The therapist burlesques basic fears in the family:

"Mother and Dad won't drop dead if you simply comment on what you see and hear."

"You must think that Mother and Dad are pretty fragile creatures. They look like pretty strong people to me."

"You seem to act, Mary, as if Joe will fall apart if you simply report on what you have observed."

By burlesquing, or by painting the picture ad absurdum, the therapist helps decrease overprotective feelings and feelings of omnipotence, thus further reducing the need for defenses.

10. The therapist decreases threat by handling loaded material with care.

a.   He handles loaded material by careful timing, going from least-loaded to most-loaded.
— He goes from a history of the past, how couples first met, what they saw in each other, to the present interaction.
— He starts with a discussion about the parents of origin and leads on to a discussion about the present parents.
— The timing of questions is done by the order in which they are asked during the history-taking:

"What did your parents do for fun?"

"How were your parents different from each other?"

"Were your parents able to disagree?"

"How did your parents disagree?"

"What do *you* do for fun?" etc.

b. The therapist switches to less loaded material when
things get hot.
— To one subject rather than another (this depends on
what in the family is the most loaded material).
— To the past rather than the present: "How did
money-handling go in your family when you were a
kid?"

c. The therapist handles loaded material by generalizing
what one expects to see in families:

"It is not unusual for families to hurt, have pain,
have problems, fight."

"When one person in a family is hurting (or angry,
or frightened) all are feeling the same way."

"When one person in a family is hurting, all share
a responsibility in that hurt."

d. The therapist handles loaded material by relating
feelings to facts.
— He asks for specificity, examples, documentation: "He
beats you sometimes? How often?" or, "He sort of
cheats? What do you mean?"
— He asks about data that patients use to support their
perceptions: "How do you know she doesn't care what
you do?" or, "What does he do that makes you feel he
is mean?"
— But he does not ignore the real things to which
patients are responding. He must be careful not to
analyze a perception without checking it out against
reality.
— Neither does he wallow in feeling or allow others to
do so. He must also keep from analyzing feelings
separate from the context of interaction.

e. He handles loaded material by using his own personal
idiom.

— He uses slang: "Dad hit the ceiling then, huh? or, "I
guess the fur flew then."

— He uses profanity, vulgarity: "All right. So he acted
like a bastard that time," or, "You must have been
mad as hell."

— He avoids pedantic words and psychiatric jargon. He
uses "self-esteem" instead of "poor sex identity";
"count" and and "valued" instead of "acceptable";
"lovable" instead of "loved," etc.

f. He handles loaded material by translating hostile
behavior and feelings:

"So you felt unlovable."

"So you felt attacked."

"So what came out of your mouth didn't match the
pain inside. How come?"

g. He handles loaded material by preventing closure on
episodes and complaints (besides, he often has
insufficient data from which to evaluate what feelings
are about): "As we go along this will become clearer," or,
"We can learn more about that."

11. Let us now move forward to seeing how the therapist
re-educates patients for adulthood, for accountability.

a. The patient constantly gives clues that he does not feel
accountable:

"I can't do it." (I am little, insignificant.)

"They won't let me do it." (Others are bigger than I
am. I am a victim.)

"You made me do it." (I fix accountability in you.)

"Yes, I do it, but can't help it. I don't know why." (I
fix accountability inside me, but I am not related to
myself.)

"I did it because I was drunk (amnesic, crazy)." (I was not me.)

"I didn't mean to do it." (I was not me.)

"I did it because I love you." (Blackmail Syndrome.)

b. The therapist uses certain techniques for restoring the patient's feeling of accountability.
   — He reminds the patient of his ability to be in charge of himself:

   "Who eats for you?"

   "Who goes to the toilet for you?"

   "You can decide, you know."

   "You don't have to rob yourself, you know." (To a patient who wants to quit school.)

   "How did it happen, if you didn't mean to do it?"

   "Others can't see your inside wish. They can only see the outward behavior which gives a clue to the wish. You have to make your wishes clear."

   "You invested that person with authority over you. Why did you give your authority away?"

   "You made an agreement with him that he would control you. Does this have to go on?"

   "What stands between you and your ability to control Mary?"
   — The therapist checks back always on pronouns to see who did what to whom. Schizophrenics, for instance, never say exactly who did what. They say: "Children shouldn't do such and such." The therapist pins the patient down: "You mean Johnnie?" The therapist makes the patient's covert accusations overt so that they can be dealt with and so that he can check if the pronouns are accurately placed.
   — The therapist deals with tattletalers:

S: (to mother) I'm going to tell on you.

Th: Now I think you want to get Ma in trouble. Does this happen at home? How come you parents are in a position where your kids can get one of you in trouble?

*   *   *   *   *   *   *

M: My husband drinks.

Th: (turns attention to what wife can report on herself) Do *you* drink?

*   *   *   *   *   *   *

D: (discrepancy watcher) He gets ten cents. I only get five cents.

Th: You want to make sure you get your share of things. That you don't get robbed or left out.
— The therapist deals with spokesmen:

"How does it happen that you have to be a spokesman for Johnny? He can speak for himself. Let's ask him about this."

"Does this go on at home? People speaking for other people? How do you suppose this came to be?"
— The therapist deals with acting-out of children (see page 164 for acting-out of adults). He doesn't turn to the parents. He asks the child, "How come?" He reminds the child that he has a choice about his behavior. He isn't a victim. He can influence his environment.

c. The patient-therapist relationship itself highlights problems of accountability.
— The patient behaves in a certain way. He acts as if he is stuck with that behavior, can't help it. If the therapist, too, treats this behavior as separate from the person, he is saying to the patient, "I expect you to have no controls." So he highlights the behavior as belonging to the person, and he sets up behavior treatment goals.

— The patient expects the therapist to be a great white father or mother from whom all things flow. He expects the therapist to take charge. The therapist does take charge, but does not treat the patient like a child or expect him to behave like one. He treats the patient like an adult and expects him to behave like an adult. He does not violate the adult label.

— The therapist is not indispensable to the patient, though he may need to think he is. He is not like the parent of the schizophrenic who says: "You can't feed yourself. You need me to live." So he doesn't give to patients in a "feeding" and "draining" kind of way. He only makes it possible for them to give to themselves and get from other family members.

12. The therapist helps the patient to see how past models influence his expectations and behavior (see page 103).

    a.   He reminds patients that they are acting from past models:

> "I would expect you to be worried about that. As you said, your dad never . . ."

> "Your mother handled money that way. How *could* you have learned other ways?"

> "Now it sounds to me as if you are giving the same kind of message to him that you saw your mother give to your dad. Yet you didn't like the way your mother and father handled things and are struggling hard to do it differently. Let's see what may be standing in your way."

    b.   The therapist openly challenges expectations: "Do you really believe that all children should be beholden to their parents?"

    c.   The therapist reminds patients that they married each other for the very qualities about which they are now complaining. "Now this is what you said you liked about your wife. I wonder why you don't like it now?"

    d.   The therapist highlights expectations by completing communication:

Th: (to Johnny) Do you like spinach?

S: No.

Th: Did you know your mother thought you did like spinach?

S: No, but I didn't want to hurt her feelings.

Th: (to mother) Did you ever ask him if he liked spinach?

M: No, I thought all men did. Pa did.

e. The therapist highlights expectations by exaggerating them: *"Your* Pa did it, so *naturally* all men do it!"

13. The therapist delineates roles and functions.

    a. The therapist recognizes roles himself, in addressing and treating a family.
      — He calls couples "Mother" and "Dad" when referring to them as parents and by their first names when referring to them as individuals or as husband and wife.
      — He then takes the oldest sib first, saying to the younger ones: "Wait a minute. You haven't arrived yet. You haven't been born!"

    b. The therapist questions patients about their roles:

      "You wear three hats—individual, marital, parental. I can see the parental, but where are the other two?"

      "Before marriage you were Miss So-and-So. What happened to her?"

      "Why do you have to get permission?"

      "Are you Daddy's wife?"

    c. The therapist can teach explicitly about roles. He lists three roles on the blackboard: individual, marital, parental. He does this so that patients will see that they have a choice as to how they will treat each other. If the therapist makes patients aware of how they are responding and shows them other ways to respond, they can then choose among these ways. Creativity in living is having a wider choice of alternatives.

14. The therapist completes gaps in communication and interprets messages.

    a.   The therapist separates the relationship part of a message from its content. Patients usually confuse the two and talk about relationships in "content" terms:
— "This coffee is no good" is a patient's way of saying, "You are no good."
— "Glasses get dirty" is a schizophrenic's way of saying, "You can't see straight."

    b.   The therapist separates comments about the self from comments about others. Patients usually confuse the two, and can't figure out which part of an interchange tells them something about the speaker and which part is addressed to them.
— "I'm tired" can be a statement about the speaker's fatigue. It can also be a question: "You too?" It can also be a request: "Help me!"
— So when the patient tells the therapist what B said, the therapist asks what the patient got out of B's message.

    c.   The therapist points out significant discrepancies in communication:

        F: I feel fine.

        Th: You look awful. How come you say you feel fine when you look awful. Can't you allow yourself to feel like Hell?

                 *   *   *   *   *   *   *

        F: (to child, whose symptom is related to the father's delinquent behavior) Be good and I'll be back soon.

Th: (to father) I think there were two parts to that message which perhaps confused her. You said to be good very loud and clear, but you did not tell her where you were going and when you would be back. Did the second message come through equally loud and clear?

d. The therapist spells out nonverbal communication:

Th: (to Johnny) You looked to your mother first, before answering. I wonder if you feel you have to get permission to speak.

Th: (To Patty, who takes her father's hand during an argument between her mother and father) Are you telling your dad that you sympathize with him?

* * * * * * *

Th: (in reference to seating pattern) You all act as though you would like to get as far away from him (me, her) as possible.

e. The therapist spells out "double-level" messages:

D: (to mother) May I go to school?

M: (to daughter) When I was a little girl, I never had an education.

Th: (to mother) Now your daughter asked you if she could go to school and I'm wondering if she got an answer from you. Should she go to school or shouldn't she?

15. In general, here are my criteria for terminating treatment.

a. Treatment is completed:
— When family members can complete transactions, check, ask.
— When they can interpret hostility.
— When they can see how others see them.
— When they can see how they see themselves.

— When one member can tell another how he manifests himself.

— When one member can tell another what he hopes, fears, and expects from him.

— When they can disagree.

— When they can make choices.

— When they can learn through practice.

— When they can free themselves from harmful effects of past models.

— When they can give a clear message, that is, be congruent in their behavior, with a minimum of difference between feelings and communication, and with a minimum of hidden messages.

b. Another set of criteria for terminating treatment is when the adult male and female as husband and wife can:

— *Be direct,* using the first person "I" and following with statements or questions which:

Criticize	Find fault
Evaluate	Report annoyance
Acknowledge an observation	Identify being puzzled

— *Be delineated,* by using language which clearly shows "I am me" and "You are you." "I am separate and apart from you and I acknowledge my own attributes as belonging to me. You are you, separate and apart from me, and I acknowledge your attributes as belonging to you."

— *Be clear,* by using questions and statements which reflect directness and the capacity to get knowledge of someone else's statements, directions, or intentions, in order to accomplish an outcome.

c. In short, treatment is completed when everyone in the therapy setting can use the first person "I" followed by an active verb and ending with a direct object.

Chapter XV

Integrating Models and Disciplines

1. Although I have described my personal conceptions and practices in this book on family therapy, I do not wish the reader to see it as just another rigid model which cannot be altered or varied. I have tried to cut through the barriers between disciplines, forms, and models, and take a look at the basic *process* that occurs in all relationships involving human beings, with particular emphasis on the therapeutic and family relationships.

2. There is nothing sacred in a formula or model. The important thing is always the understanding and use of the formula in the here and now. Form is *not* the same as process.

    a. Process implies movement. It is dynamic, not static.

    b. Process focuses not on the activity *per se,* but on the carrying on of the activity.

    c. Process is more a matter of "how" than of "what"; form and content are more matters of "what" than of "how."

    d. One of the reasons why diagnostic labels can become

damaging is that they can easily become self-fulfilling prophecies, tending to freeze process into outcome.

e. Process avoids dichotomies, since a person can be X at one moment in time and Y at another moment.

f. Process is best described in verbs ending in -*ing*.

3. The basic process which occurs in every relationship, regardless of content, structure, or form, is:

a. an encounter

b. between two people

c. at a particular moment in time.

4. The future of human relations disciplines and modalities lies in the integration of their various partial views of man in relation to the five basic parts of the self, which are:

a. the mind

b. the body

c. the spiritual part of the self

d. the report of the senses (the interaction between mind and body), and

e. interaction with others (social relationships).

5. All of us operate within multiple relationship systems, and our self-concepts and self-images are derived from the context of the system we are in at any particular moment in time. This means that identity is dynamic, constantly changing, and the individual has myriad potentials and contingency possibilities that are only neglected through prohibitions and sanctions preventing self-exploration and change. The limited individual has a limited self-image, which he derives from a limited context that prevents growth.

6. If one approaches therapy from an integrational viewpoint, it becomes clear that many fields not labeled as "human relations" disciplines had much to say about parts of the human gestalt long before human relations fields emerged. In my therapy and training, I make use of principles and ideas gleaned from the disciplines of dance, drama, religion, medicine, communications, education, speech, the behavioral sciences—and the physical sciences, from which the "systems concept" (on which my practice is based) first derived.* Integration, in theory and practice, of all the tools available to people for their growth is necessary before we begin to deal in fact with the "total person."

7. Proscribed, rigid psychotherapeutic practices are inadequate to meet the constantly changing growth needs of human beings. The truth of this statement is obvious from the points I have stressed throughout this book, namely:

   a. the need for the individual to observe himself in interaction, including the part he plays in the family system,

   b. the need to realize how his behavior and self-concept is circumscribed by the system itself, and

   c. the need for therapeutic reinforcement to make this knowledge available to family members and help them experience and practice new interactional behaviors.

8. In my own treatment sessions, I tailor my treatment to meet the needs of the family.

   a. I range from an intake interview that may last an hour and a half to sessions which last several or more hours. More recently, I have relied increasingly on "marathon" sessions, which means spending a weekend or longer with one or several families in order to have continuous

---

*For a complete explanation of the systems concept, see Watzlawick, P., Beavin, J., and Jackson, D., *Pragmatics of Human Communication,* New York: W. W. Norton, 1967.

contact in a variety of contexts. In other words, *time* is flexible and variable.

b. I see families and individuals in my office, outdoors, in their homes, in their places of work and recreation; i.e., anyplace it seems likely that we can experience new contexts and relationships. I visit the school and nursery, if indicated. In short, *place* is flexible and variable.

c. Once I have seen the family together enough to have a good, comprehensive understanding of the total family system, I can see a particular family member in an individual session, or see certain family dyads or triads, or shift sessions from seeing one or two at a time to seeing the whole family together again, often in a single interview. I vary the sessions according to the need and my analysis of the family system. Often, I see more than one family together. In other words, the pattern of *persons* seen is flexible and variable.

d. At times, I find it helpful to utilize a co-therapist or more than one co-therapist, either of the same sex or the opposite sex. Therefore, the pattern of *therapists* involved is flexible and variable.

e. In addition to varying techniques and time patterns, I use many invaluable mechanical aids in therapy and training. I use both audio and video tape recorders to give instant feedback, or review earlier interactional episodes, or take a picture of the person who doubts that he looks angry or depressed or is giving other unconscious, nonverbal messages to others in interaction. I have increasingly utilized dancing, body movement exercises, music, art, drama, and games in order to provide the family with varying experiences in touching, seeing, hearing, feeling, and expressing. In short, *techniques* and *tools* for experiencing are flexible and variable.

9. Naturally, none of these techniques has been established as "ideal" or "the most desirable," and many new aids other than those I have described will doubtless be developed in the future. The important point is that whatever techniques are used, the focus should be on providing a new growth experience for the family or the individual. This means that

the therapist must be a *person* and a peer to the family and not a godlike figure who tries to hold himself aloof from the relationship system.

10. The therapeutic modus operandi, which governs how much the therapist permits himself to become involved and in what way, depends heavily on the therapist's models and beliefs about:

    a. what causes illness,

    b. what makes illness go away, and

    c. what makes people grow.

11. One can visualize today's psychotherapy as being based generally on one of two models:

    a. the medical model, or

    b. the growth model.

12. In the medical model, the cause of illness is believed to have its locus in the patient himself. It is believed that the illness is removed by destroying its source within the patient. Growth is expected to occur spontaneously once the cause of the illness is removed, thereby releasing pent-up energy for growth. In this model, the use of touch or closeness by the therapist is irrelevant, since the problem is within the patient. The psychoanalytic model is a perfect example of the medical model because here the patient lies on the couch, speaks from his "innermost" mind, and does not even have eye contact with the therapist. If the analyst adheres strictly to "non-directive, patient-oriented" techniques, even verbal contact is strictly limited. The assumption is that "I, the therapist, do nothing to stimulate you, so everything you feel and do is inherent in you." Since it is impossible *not* to communicate, however, this assumption is a myth.

13. The growth model is based on the notion that people's behavior changes through process and that the process is represented by transactions with other people and with the

various parts of oneself. Illness is believed to be an appropriate communicative response to a dysfunctional system or context existing within the individual and other people in the family context. It is therefore believed that health develops when the system is changed to permit healthy responses and communication. The therapist, being an integral part of the therapeutic system, is intimately involved in the transactions, and anything he or she may offer the patient or patients to expedite learning and exchange is utilized to help the patient grow within the context of the relationship.

14. If one uses the growth model, one must be willing to be more experimental and spontaneous than many therapists are. The necessity of flexibility in technique and approach, including particularly direct, intimate contact between patient and therapist, is thought to be basic.

   a. In growth therapy, techniques are not utilized to accomplish specific goals, such as increasing the father's yearly earnings or making sure that junior goes to college.

   b. Growth therapy is based on the premise that people can be taught to be congruent, to speak directly and clearly, and to communicate their feelings, thoughts, and desires accurately in order to be able to deal with what is.

15. To compare these models in action, let us imagine, for example, that a patient were to ask how the therapist has fun.

   a. In the medical model, the question would be considered irrelevant.

   b. In the growth model, the question would be considered a legitimate request for information.

16. In the growth model, the therapist makes the point by his *own* behavior that there is nothing which cannot be dealt with openly and honestly, nor is there any substitute in therapy or any human relationship for a human being's learning to use himself and his own personality—not only

using himself to influence others but, when appropriate, letting go and being influenced by others.

17. The therapist, because he is a person intimately involved in the relationship system, provides an example for growth, either positively or negatively.

    a. The vision presented by the traditional analyst is that of withdrawal, non-involvement, non-commitment, and the virtual elimination of looking, talking, and touching as effective means of communication in relationship.

    b. In the growth model, the therapist sets the example of an active, learning, fallible human being who is willing to cope honestly and responsibly with whatever confronts him, including his own vulnerabilities.

18. In order to learn and to demonstrate what happens to an individual's behavior when he operates within the context of one of the two models described, I have in recent years made increasing use of games—both in family therapy and in training professionals in various human relations disciplines. The major games I have developed for this purpose are:

    a. the simulated family,

    b. family systems games, and

    c. communication games.

The Simulated Family

1. The Bateson group, working in Palo Alto in 1954, came upon the notion that families are constrained by redundant behavioral patterns that occur over and over again outside of the family's awareness. In attempting to demonstrate this by utilizing role-playing among the members of the group (Bateson, Jackson, Haley, and Weakland), they were surprised to find themselves developing strong feelings in relation to the behaviors they were merely acting out in the role of a particular "family" member. Further, they were

able to show that, by following certain simple rules, they could simulate, for example, the family of a chronic schizophrenic patient to such a degree that the recording of these sessions sent for "blind" diagnosis to various other investigators in the country was considered to be a tape of a real schizophrenic family. Even the voices of the researchers (who were well known to the other investigators) were not recognized, although no voice change had been intended by the so-called "role-players."

2. I have had experience now with utilizing "simulated family" techniques with hundreds of different audiences and with many different professional groups, from physicians to social workers, teachers, and nurses. One comment should be made about the use of games for training purposes. A common reaction of professionals who have not participated in such games is that it is just "role-playing" and therefore unreal. In all of my experience in using these games with many groups across the country, I have never encountered a person who did not, once involved in a game system, develop vivid "gut reactions" to the roles he played, particularly those roles which are contrary to his own self-image. It is very common for someone to say, after a particular game, "Now I know how Mrs. X feels and can sympathize with her ulcer problem! This sounds just like her. After five minutes of it, my own stomach is churning."

3. On one memorable occasion, a young social worker played the identified-patient daughter in a particular simulated family, while a general physician, interested in family therapy, was her simulated father. At the end of about forty minutes of family interaction, the "daughter" stood up, threw her arms around the older man and stated, "I really love you!" and he, with tears streaming down his face, stated, "It's the first time I have ever really felt what I missed in not having a daughter."

4. Naturally, the technique of the simulated family is not used only to teach therapists but is invaluable in teaching real families about themselves. This can be done in two primary ways:

a. The therapist can have family members simulate each
    other's behaviors. For example, mother may behave as
    she thinks father does, while father may play the part of
    his daughter, and the son may act out his conception of
    his mother's behavior.

b. The therapist can have the family members play
    themselves in a simulated situation, i.e., one that the
    therapist constructs from his understanding of their
    particular family system. For example, in a scapegoating
    family, the members may be required to act out a drama
    in which they are to pretend they are a different family,
    one in which little Johnny is the favorite. Mother is the
    one who is always being picked on by the other family
    members, and she puts up with it by being a martyr.
    The family can then be made acquainted with their
    behavior by the use of audio-visual tape, which is played
    back to them, and both family and therapist discuss how
    different or how similar various family members'
    behaviors were in relation to their usual behaviors.

Systems Games:

1. A very useful tool for both training and therapy is what I
    call "family systems games." I developed these on the basis
    of my observation over a period of time that all interactional
    systems can be classified as either *open systems* or *closed
    systems*.

    a. Closed systems are those in which every participating
        member must be very cautious about what he or she
        says. The principal rule seems to be that everyone is
        supposed to have the same opinions, feelings, and
        desires, whether or not this is true. In closed systems,
        honest self-expression is impossible, and if it does occur,
        the expression is viewed as deviant or "sick" or "crazy"
        by the other members of the group or family.
        Differences are treated as dangerous, a situation that
        results in one or more members having to figuratively
        "be dead to themselves" if they are to remain in the
        system. The limitations placed on individual growth and
        health in such a group is obvious, and I have found that
        emotional or behavioral disturbance is a certain sign

that the disturbed person is a member of a closed family system.

    b.   An open system permits honest self-expression for the participating members. In such a group or family, differences are viewed as natural, and open negotiation occurs to resolve such differences by "compromise," "agreement to disagree," "taking turns," etc. In open systems, the individual can say what he feels and thinks and can negotiate for reality and personal growth without destroying himself or the others in the system.

2. Through the use of five basic "rules" of interactional patterns played by the original family triad (father, mother, and child) or by trainees taking these roles, I discovered that it is possible to simulate almost any family system, closed or open, and to learn in the process.

    a.   The first interactional rule dictates that a person is to handle differences by eliminating himself. In other words, he always *agrees* with others in the system regardless of how he really feels.

    b.   The second rule is that one may handle differences by eliminating the others, by always *disagreeing,* finding fault, and blaming.

    c.   In the third rule, one eliminates both self and other by preaching and/or rationalizing, being careful to keep a mask of non-movement and non-emotional involvement so that differences are supposedly handled on a "reasonable" basis.

    d.   In the fourth rule, one eliminates self, other, and the context by being irrelevant, changing the subject, etc., so that both self and other find it impossible to negotiate differences openly.

    e.   The fifth rule permits the inclusion of both self and other in the system, i.e., a person negotiates openly and clearly and permits others to do the same.

3. On the basis of these five rules, I devised five sets of games to simulate, by shifting the component parts, any system of interaction.

a.   The first set is called *rescue games,* in which rules
     number one, two, and four are played, i.e., one member
     of the original family triad always agrees, one always
     disagrees, and the third is always irrelevant. In most
     interactional systems, the same person plays by the same
     rule most of the time. Who plays by which rule is
     variable—i.e., Father can be the agreer, Mother the
     disagreer, and the child, the subject-changer; or Mother
     can be the irrelevant one, the child the agreer, and
     Father the disagreer. This pattern of interaction is very
     common in families that produce a schizophrenic
     member.

b.   The second set of games is called *coalition games,* which
     are based on rules one and two. In other words, two
     people always agree and the third disagrees or two
     disagree and one agrees. The implications for people
     caught in this game are obvious. It requires some
     "disturbed behavior" in order for a person to disagree
     with two people when one of those is agreeing and one is
     disagreeing, or for a person to agree with two people
     who are disagreeing, etc.

c.   The third set of games, called *lethal games,* is made up
     completely of rule one. In such a system, everyone
     agrees with everyone else, at the expense of his own
     needs and satisfactions. This is a common interactional
     pattern in families that develop a high incidence of
     psychosomatic illness.

d.   The fourth set of games is called *"proper and correct"
     games.* Here everyone tries to be reasonable, regardless
     of how they feel.

e.   The fifth set of games is composed entirely of rule five,
     and I call it *growth vitality games.* In such a system,
     each person includes self and others in interaction by
     expressing himself and also permitting others to express
     themselves.

4.   It is obvious that the *growth vitality game* does not exist on
     the same level as the first four games. The first four games
     are survival games, and the fifth simply occurs on the
     content reality level rather than on the survival level. In

such a game, people can *either* agree *or* disagree, in accordance with their experiential reality, and still remain a part of the system.

5. I use these games in treatment and in training. They are invaluable in three major ways:

   a. They help real or simulated "families" to see and understand the nature of their own family system.

   b. They permit the family and the trainee to experience *new* interactional patterns (while experiencing new behaviors in their individual reaction patterns).

   c. By having a family play the full sequence of games, they can not only identify where they *are* but also where it is possible to go. By making the systems explicit and ending with a "growth vitality game," families and professional trainees can *experience* the *movement* from a pathological system of interaction to a growth-producing one.

6. These games are not fixed and invariable. Within the general framework, the parts and variables can be shifted and rearranged to suit the needs of the occasion.

   a. Instructions are usually necessary, such as assigning the roles and describing what the participants must do (e.g., to always agree with whatever is said without using the words "I agree"). I usually assign a task for the group to carry out, such as, "Plan something you can do together as a family," or, "Using these rules, tell each other how you feel." From there on, they carry the ball any way they can.

   b. Sometimes I join in as a participant; sometimes, I observe. Sometimes, I interrupt or give new instructions, whispered to individuals or aloud to the whole family. Sometimes, I whisper a switch in role to one member, so the family can see what happens to a system when one member changes his rules of behavior without advising the other members.

c. Of course, it is of great importance that the family discuss their feelings and thoughts and reactions during and/or after the game. Strong emphasis is placed on "gut feelings," i.e., the physical, body reactions to the role being played. For example, when an individual must always agree, he may experience body tenseness, tight stomach, deep anger, etc. One who "always disagrees" may experience body heat, shaking, and headache. The "super reasonable" one may feel dry. The "irrelevant one" may feel "crazy as a loon."

Communication Games:

1. The third major category of games I have developed is a series of various interactional techniques that are great for teaching people to communicate more effectively and congruently. To date, the *communication games* have been used primarily with dyads, but it is not difficult to imagine expanding the idea to incorporate varied operational techniques.

2. I hit upon these games due to my repeated observation that when a person delivers an incongruent or mixed message, he or she usually is "out of touch" with the listener, in that little skin and eye contact occurs. I discovered after some experimentation that people find it almost impossible to send out an incongruent message if they have skin and/or steady eye contact with the listener. In my efforts to teach my patients and trainees to improve their communications, I developed the following techniques. They are meant to be used generally as a *series* of interactions, to show people concretely and experientially what happens when they do or do not look, touch, and speak in a congruent manner.

a. I place two persons (mother and father, father and child, two trainees, etc.) back to back and ask them to talk. This is similar in form to some communications at home, with the wife in the kitchen cooking while her husband tries to discuss finances with her.

b. Then I turn them around face to face and have them "eyeball" each other without touching or talking. A great deal is learned when discussing this interaction, about the assumptions a person makes about the other's thoughts and feelings when communication is verbally and sensorily constrained.

c. I then have the couple "eyeball" and touch each other without talking.

d. They then are asked to touch (e.g., hold hands) with their eyes closed and without talking.

e. They then "eyeball" and talk without touching.

f. Finally, I have the couple talk and touch and "eyeball" and *try to argue with each other.* They find that it is impossible. They either enjoy the effort or are forced to pull back physically and divert their eyes to get angry. It is also very difficult to deliver an incongruent message when one is talking, touching, and looking at the listener.

3. The most important part of these games is the therapist's interventions and the discussions during and after the series, about the couple's feelings, responses, and gut (bodily) reactions in relation to themselves, the other, and the interaction itself.

4. A final variation I will describe here is what I call the "blind walk." This technique involves having one person (e.g., the wife) take another (husband, child, etc.) on a walk while the second party keeps his or her eyes closed. I ask the person "in charge" to make the walk as interesting as possible (for example, having the "blind" person sit, stand, feel objects, etc.) and to use his/her body freely to direct the partner without possible injury. They are not permitted to talk during the walk. Afterwards, we discuss their feelings—fears, doubts, sense of trust, enjoyment, etc. For couples with serious "trust" and "dependence" problems in their relationship, this game can be particularly useful.

5. All of the games described can be helpful or useless in therapy, depending on the ability of the therapist to enter

into the relationship system openly and flexibly. One must, above all, show the enthusiasm and personal commitment necessary to engage one's patients in the spirit of learning, experimentation, and serious appraisal necessary to make the games a vivid new experience in interaction.

6. I repeat once again that these games are not to be reified or labeled as techniques applicable only in the "innovative freedom of sunny California." They can be added to, abbreviated, or revised in accordance with the therapist's idiosyncratic personality and his clients' particular needs, problems, and wishes. They are the forms, not the process, of therapy. The *process* still—and always—is the *relationship between you and me, here and now.*

PART FOUR: WHEN I MEET A PERSON

People have often asked me how I look at people and what I see when I look. Many times what I think people are really asking is what kind of beliefs I have about people. I will try to answer this in a way that I think might help people understand more about some of the things that I do when I'm working with people. I will treat this in an extemporaneous fashion, trying to put together what I do as thoughts occur to me. I am quite aware that many of the ways I feel and things I do may not be all that's there, but I will share with you the best that I know at this point.

I would like to start with what goes on in me when I think about using myself as a helper to another person. In the first place, the person and his family—because I almost always think in the family context—would not be coming to me unless they had some kind of pain or some kind of problem that they wanted to solve. In some way I feel them as having said to themselves (or having been told by someone else), "We've reached the end of our ability to cope, and we are searching for

---

This chapter is based on an article by the same title that appeared in *Tidings of Comfort and Joy*, edited by Robert S. Spitzer, M.D. (Palo Alto: Science and Behavior Books, 1975).

some way to cope better." People don't always put it in that language. Sometimes they only say, "I hurt" or "Somebody is doing something wrong." I hear it as a search for a new ability to cope better with their lives, and to have more joy and pleasure, less pain, and perhaps more productivity.

I see all people as representations of life, in whatever form that happens to be. When people are in need or are having some kind of problem, their manifestation of themselves—the way they look and sound and talk—can be pretty ugly, pretty beautiful, or pretty painful. Underneath all this I see the living human who, I feel, would use himself or herself differently if he or she were in touch with the life that he or she is and has. So with every human being that I encounter, I mentally take off his or her outside and try to see the inside, which is that piece of the self that I call self-worth or self-esteem, and to which I have given the affectionate name "pot." This "pot" is searching for some way of manifesting itself, and I meet a person with that awareness. There is in the person that which probably he or she has not touched. That person not only hasn't touched it—he or she doesn't even know it's there. I know it's there. This conviction in me is so strong that it is a given for me. I never ask *if* that person has life; I ask only how it can be touched.

Yesterday I did an interview with a family which is fresh in my mind at the moment. What I am going to try to do is describe in the best way I can what happened between the family and me. I'll supply my understanding of what was going on in me, and how I used that understanding to reach the self-worth of each member of the family. This family had an adult male and an adult female who were husband and wife. These two adults were also father and mother of five children, the oldest eighteen and the youngest five. Of course, they had some kind of problem or they wouldn't have come in for treatment. That part was also obvious.

To start off, I was not so much concerned with a particular problem as with trying to understand and learn about how each person in this family lived his or her life, both with the others and with himself or herself. For me, there are always two lives going on all the time—mine with myself, and mine with the other people who are significant to me. When I met this family, I didn't know what I was going to find. I did not know how these particular family members were going to manifest themselves; I only knew that they were hurting and that they had something in them that could be touched and developed and that could grow.

The first thing I did was to meet each one. Something that I am quite aware of is that people aren't usually related to themselves as people of worth. I feel that no changes can be made in people unless they begin to feel themselves as having worth, and that I as the therapist become the first means by which a person comes in touch with his or her own feeling of worth. My meeting with this family was the beginning of this. I extended my hand to the husband-father, and subsequently did the same with all the rest of the family.

I would like to say a little bit about what it was like for me when I did that. In the first place—and you might think along with me—suppose you are someone I am just meeting. You are with a group of people, perhaps members of your family, and I stand in front of you and reach out my hand to you at arm level. As I reach for your hand and you give it to me, I feel a connection. At that moment in time, I am looking at you; I am in touch with your skin feelings and my skin feelings and for that moment there is no one else in the world except you and me. You are the receiver of my full attention at that moment. You can feel that what I am connecting with is your personhood, and I feel that I am giving mine to you. A smile accompanies this, and my smile is saying "hello" to you and to your life as a representation of all life. This kind of experience makes it possible for me to feel that I am connected with another form of life, another manifestation of life—yours. I regard life manifestation as the basis of what personhood is all about.

As I do this with each member of your family, I am also aware within myself that I am enjoying having the contact—full contact—which in some way also affirms me. I am a living being connected with another living being. It is like the platform or the base from which we are going to go. This is why I do not start out my treatment session with a discussion of the problem, but rather make this basic connection on a human level with everyone. Of course, people are coming in for some help; if they knew what sort of help they needed, they would probably be doing it themselves and not seeking me. They have come to the end of their coping and they want some help, but probably all that they are aware of is that they have pain.

As I am making this first contact with them, I am listening to their responses to me. In a few moments, I will hear responses from the people to each another. I begin to get a feeling for what they have done, how they have used their experiences from the time they popped out of the womb until now. Some of you may be familiar with the stances I use for shorthand purposes—the ways in which people communicate with one another, the responses I have labeled as *placating, blaming, super-reasonable, irrelevant,* and *flow.* At the beginning of treatment I do not expect the family to display many flow responses, because the fact that they haven't arrived at that point is probably one of the reasons they are coping in the way that they are. I also want to underscore the fact that I see the people in front of me as doing the very best they can with what they have learned; and I believe that what they have learned represents the best way they know how to survive. Some of you may be aware that I have translated the various kinds of responses into body positions. Within a few moments, I am making mental pictures of the people in front of me and translating them into physical postures that represent their ways of communicating.

For example, in the family I saw yesterday, I saw the man as making super-reasonable responses. That meant that in my imagination he was standing there very erect, with very little movement, speaking in a rather monotonous way. I saw the woman kneeling before him in a placating position, but at the same time—behind her back—pointing an accusing finger at him. I saw the oldest daughter standing and super-reasonable like her father, looking at neither parent but with one finger barely poking out, pointing at her father. I saw the next girl very deliberately and in a very obvious way pointing her finger at her mother. The next child was a boy. I saw him standing very close to his mother and placating her. Then I saw the next child as giving out irrelevant responses by moving all over the place and not being able to fix on anyone. I also saw the youngest child, a five-year-old girl, as being irrelevant.

As I saw these pictures in my mind, it was important to respect them as representing the best ways that these people had developed to cope. Their ways of placating, blaming, and being super-reasonable or irrelevant had formed a system which meant that no one in the family could really approach the personhood of another. They were likely to mishear one another; they were seeing roles rather than real people. So my search and my efforts would be directed to helping these people to become real with one another. I looked at this family, and my insides felt them respond to my contact. Full contact, by the way, carries the message of caring—caring in a deep, personal sense—and I regard that contact as a vital basis for developing any changes. There has to be high trust. If people in the family group do not find me trustworthy, I don't think we are going to be able to effect any changes.

I remember that as I entered the room yesterday, the family was spread around on chairs, looking very much like targets on a rifle range. A table was in front of them. As I looked at this scene, I felt that it would be very awkward to work in this context. I feel very strongly that where people are sitting (far apart or close together) and the way they are sitting is very important. I need to make the place where I work comfortable— that is, to arrange it so that I can see everybody. I place myself within arm's length of each person. There must be enough space for me and the other people to move about. This space is necessary because sometimes I will have family members work in pairs, or I will do "sculpturing" or some other kind of activity that requires space. A table or other obstacle makes movement difficult. Yesterday, I moved the table and fixed it so that I was no more than a small step away from making touch contact with everyone in the group.

The little five-year-old was on my right. At one point I noticed that she was moving back a little bit. By this time I had the feeling that she was regarded as the troublemaker in the family and was rather on the outside. I slipped my hand around her back—she had a nice, round back—and I found myself feeling the enjoyment of touching her. I think she felt this as a message of encouragement to be a part of the group. Throughout the interview there was much more of this.

One can touch in all kinds of ways. In training therapists, I have told them that to develop "eyes and ears" in their fingers is important. People in families are touching all the time—slapping, pushing, shoving, holding. I'm sure all of you know that touches have different meanings. So it isn't a matter of giving a touch; it's a matter of the message in the touch. I referred earlier to developing trust. That means that the atmosphere, through trust, has to be such that people can begin to talk about what I call "unspeakable things"—the things that are close to their hearts—what they worry about, what they fear, and what they hope for. I don't know if I can state this strongly enough. To me, that people *do* say what was once unspeakable is much more important than *what* they say. Sometimes it takes a little while for people to get the feeling that whatever they say can be heard and understood. It does not have to be run through any censorship system about what is right. I don't know of any way to help a person get to himself or herself unless that person can let out whatever is there. That is not a usual thing in this society, as many of you doubtlessly know. But to create the context and the working way for change to take place, it seems to me that no one can be penalized in any way for what he or she says—at least not by me. Instead, I must take whatever someone says and make this a living account of where the person is at that moment. What that person says must be understood by him or her as well as by everyone else. This means that a great deal of clarifying must go on so that a family can understand what each member is really trying to say.

As yesterday's interview proceeded, I put a question to each person in the family: "What do you hope will happen to you as a result of your coming here?" I suppose the usual question a therapist might ask is, "What is the problem?" I *am* interested in finding out where people are locked in, but I also feel that my way of asking about this and what I ask helps the person to center more on himself or herself. It also goes a little way toward diminishing the negative "vibes" that are usually there—usually in some form of "Well, if he or she were better, I would be better," or something of that sort.

In this instance I started out with the oldest daughter. At this moment I don't know why I did, except that at the time it seemed to be the right place to start. She said that she would like to see the family "not fight so much." I went on to her sister, who said the same thing. I asked other family members if they had noticed that there was a lot of fighting going on. Everyone acknowledged this. The next picture that emerged in my mind was of the two older girls fighting with one another. It seemed at that point that they were the focus around which the family's problems centered. The argument was that if these two girls didn't fight, then the family would be better. What this introduced was how the people in this family would be comfortable about expressing their anger. When I put my question to the father, his answer was that his family needed to be educated on things they had previously not known.

Because I like to make an "alive" picture as quickly as possible, it seemed natural at that point to ask the two older girls to get up and point their fingers at each other in order to see what other family members did when this happened. I find that words are more useful when there is a picture; I call this "sculpturing" or "posturing." I found that when I asked the two girls to point at each other, they were very reluctant to do so. They talked about how they fought, but actually putting themselves in the position of doing it made it more real. They seemed embarrassed.

One of the important things that I try to do is help people to be free (I am using "free" in the sense of having options and choices). I encourage people to start playing with new ideas about their behavior. I give them support to break through their taboos. Since the two girls were embarrassed, I stood behind the girl who seemed most embarrassed and supported her, standing close to her back and taking her arm and helping it to go out in a pointing direction. Then I did the same thing for the other girl. I was essentially taking the first step toward breaking this family's rule that you shouldn't be angry. This then led to the matter of what the others in the family do when there is fighting. Here were the two girls standing and pointing at each other, and everyone in the family had seen this before. My next question to the husband-father was, "What do you do when this happens?" He said he tried to tell the girls to stop, but it didn't do any good. I had him come up with his finger pointing and when he saw that this did no good either, he dropped his arm and sat down. One of the girls said the wife-mother "came on a little stronger," so I had her come in with her finger pointing. I asked some of the other children what usually happened. They said they tried to stay out of it. The oldest boy now went to his mother's side, so he came in like an auxiliary father, trying to help her with the problem between the two girls.

This kind of sculpturing has value because it makes explicit what is going on. It also brings the present (but not acknowledged) family process picture to life. This picture is not to show how bad people are, but to help them see what is going on. There is oftentimes a good bit of humor in this. I remember at one point asking the oldest girl to put out her finger. Her hand was a little wobbly, so I supported it and asked her to make believe there really was a pistol at the end of her hand. Lighthearted things like this tend to help neutralize the negative self-worth effect and to increase the ability of the person to look and see. For me, it is very important to make the separation between the person, his or her values, and how he or she is using himself or herself. I am bringing people in touch with the various ways they use themselves as well as with how they can use themselves differently. I do this in ways that raise their feelings of self-worth.

People often ask me if I feel drained after an interview. My answer is "No." I *would* get drained if I kept asking myself all kinds of questions like "Am I doing it right? Will people love me? Am I going to come out with a cure?" If I started to do that (which I call "potting myself"), I would lose track of the system and process that are going on and I would be on *my* story rather than the story of the family.

This leads me now to something else. I consider myself the leader of the *process* in the interview but *not* the leader of the *people*. I check out everything I do with them before I do it. I am a strong leader for the process. This is based on the fact that I am the one who knows what the process I am trying to produce is all about. I want to help people to become their own designers of their own choice-making; before they can do that, they need to be free to take risks. My checking out with them their willingness to undertake something new is a very important piece of this interaction and alerts them to the experience of taking risks. If I have something to offer you, I need to tell you about it; I need to show you; I need to ask you if what I offer has any value to you. What is important is that if I am introducing something new to you and I ask you too soon if you are willing to do it—that is, before I have gotten your understanding, trust, and willingness to take risks—then you will not be in a place where you feel that you can take a chance.

People often say to me, "Well, what if something you do backfires?" I answer, "That's not unusual." It is what happens in life when you try something that doesn't work. You have some choices after that. You can call yourself bad names for trying it out, or you can use it as a life experience and learn from it. Nothing backfired in yesterday's interview because it seemed that I was in the flow and had nice things going. That is the whole point. As a therapist, I try to be aware of what is happening and keep it flowing rather than try continually to keep score of what is right or wrong.

This might be a good place to say that when I am speaking to a family, I am not trying to solve a specific problem such as should they get a divorce or should they have a baby. I am working to help people find a different kind of coping process. I do not see myself as wise enough to know what is the best thing for a person to do. Should the wife ask her mother-in-law to leave? Should she *demand* that she leave? Should the wife leave her husband if the mother-in-law doesn't leave? These kinds of questions are not mine to answer. My task is to help each person with his or her own coping so that he or she can decide to do the things that work for him or her.

In yesterday's family, it came out that the second girl had occasionally talked of committing suicide. A lot of hate responses were going on between her and her mother. Instead of responding to that hate, I read in my insides that these two people wanted very much to get a connection with each other but there were all kinds of barriers between them. I had learned earlier that the wife-mother had viewed this particular child as having the same problems she had had, and was feeling very bad about seeing them in her child. Apparently the mother was trying to solve the problems in herself by trying to solve them in her daughter. This, of course, was why these two could not get together.

I asked the two of them to move toward each other, because by this time the trust level was sufficiently established so that they would be willing to take this risk. First I had them move to where they could see each other clearly, approximately at arm's length, and then I had them look at each other. I then had them close their eyes and I asked each of them to tell me what she saw. This was very interesting. The wife-mother said she saw a little baby whom she hadn't cared for very well, and that she was feeling very guilty. She began to sob a little. When I asked the daughter what she had seen, she said first that she just saw her mother. Then, after her mother had spoken, the girl said, "Well, she always sees me as a baby."

What I was aware of at this point was that these two were not seeing each other as they really were at this point in time; they were seeing each other in terms of past experience. If they didn't change, they would continue to see each other in this way and problems between them would escalate.

One of the criticisms that the daughter had made earlier was that her mother always treated her like a little baby. After this disclosure, I pointed out to the mother that she was indeed seeing this thirteen-year-old as a baby. Then, after asking the mother her age, I pointed out to the daughter that she was seeing a thirty-six-year-old person. I stated that there were these two *ladies* (I used that word), Cynthia and June, who were looking at each other. I wondered out loud if they would see each other as Cynthia and June. Then I asked them to look again and tell me, after shutting their eyes, what they saw.

They were being what I call "brought up to date." As June (the mother) spoke, she said she saw this thirteen-year-old who was attractive and that it was a whole new awareness for her. The daughter said she saw her mother and the look in her eyes, which seemed to be a look of caring for her and which she liked. Both of them at that point said they felt a whole lot different about one another.

The family then moved on to another situation involving the older daughter and her father. She was almost eighteen, and her father was still insisting that she come home early. It turned out that this man, because of his psychological and physical problems, had not yet come to a place where he could see himself as supporting his family by his work alone. His wife was working from 2:30 in the afternoon until midnight or so, which meant that the bulk of the management of the family was in the hands of the husband. He had worked out with the older daughter that she cooked dinner. Apparently she did the shopping, too. He demanded that she come home early, which she felt was an affront—a kind of invasion.

I asked these two to sit in front of one another and just try to hear one another. I guided their listening and helped them to see that they were not talking to each other in terms of what the other was saying but only in terms of how each wanted to control the other. After this, it seemed as though both the daughter and her father had come to a new understanding.

It was quite clear at this point that both the husband and wife were very fearful about what would happen to their children. Another piece of information that came out was that both of them had parents who had left them early. They were both brought up by grandparents who apparently were very anxious about them. This anxiety was transferred. Without this being clear before, most of the children in the family heard the parents' efforts to care for them as something against them. They had not been in touch with this other part. At the same time, the parents had been hearing their children as being quarrelsome and unappreciative. We were able to make some new connections.

Throughout the interview, my mental picture was one of content flowing out and connections being made. Using myself in a very active way, I could pick out times (as with the mother and daughter) to make a new connection. During the flow of touching in the family, the mother said that she hoped that her youngest son would hug her. When he came home, he only gave her a "little old hug" and she always felt cheated. The whole question of affection in the family and how people could be affectionate was brought up. This had had a taboo on it. At the end of the interview—because I was enjoying the family and feeling affectionate feelings toward them—it was natural for me to hug the members of the family. Just after I hugged the mother and went to the two sisters, I heard a little snickering by the two boys, aged eighteen and twelve. What crossed my mind was that these two boys were at a period where it might be awkward for them to engage in this kind of thing even though I felt they wanted some kind of expression of affection from me. When I turned to the first of them, I commented that I had heard the snickering and that maybe this was a bit much for them, but I wanted them to know that I had these feelings. Then I gave them each an extra-warm handshake and a pat on the shoulder, trying to respect where they were at that point and at the same time to convey my message. What was interesting also was that the father was the last one I went to; I had the feeling that he was almost standing in line waiting and would be willing to hug but couldn't quite ask. When I made the overture to him, he came readily to be hugged. I know that men very often have had experiences in the past where it wasn't manly to have such feelings, and so I found myself telling the father that Bob Hope had spoken so many years ago about an individual who "had not been cuddled and so he curdled." This helped the father to put an acceptable face on this display of affection.

The observers watching the family yesterday could see life begin to be much more evident in these people. I am aware right now that when I think about my treatment sessions, I think of them as experiences in human contact which for me— without being in any sense mystical—create a feeling that I have had a journey and an adventure with other live beings. I hope that as a result of our journey, the people are feeling more alive, more lovable, more hopeful, more creative, and are seeing new ways to use themselves and to connect with each other. Often, I see people only one time. My hope is that every interview will result in a new window for each person to look through with the result of feeling better about himself or herself and gaining the ability to do things more creatively with other members of his or her family. This is really what I mean by saying that I am dealing with a coping process rather than a problem-solving process.

I would like to return to my use of the communication stances as aids to developing changes in the coping process. I mentioned the four stances which I expect to see in some combination with all of the people who are experiencing problems in coping. Placating, blaming, being super-reasonable, and being irrelevant all appeared in yesterday's family. Incidentally, one of the things I have become increasingly conscious of is that the American dream about what a person should be really fits my category of the super-reasonable response. This response is: "For goodness sake, don't show any feeling!" This to me is sad, but it is also true.

At this point I will digress a moment and state that the stances are not rigid and unchangeable. Each of these ways of communicating can be "renovated." If you are handling your responses by placating, one of the ravages going on within you is that you keep giving yourself messages that you don't count for very much. However, if you know how, you can renovate this ability to be tender and bring it into your awareness instead of just feeling an automatic given that you always have to please everyone.

Renovated blaming becomes your ability to stand up for yourself. Everyone needs to be able to do that, but you must do it realistically and consciously rather than automatically.

Renovated super-reasonableness becomes the creative use of your intelligence. Using your intelligence is delightful; but if it is used only to protect yourself, it becomes rather boring and unfulfilling.

Renovated irrelevancy becomes your ability to be spontaneous and to give yourself a new direction in awareness and in reality.

In any case, in dealing with a super-reasonable person—like the father in yesterday's family—the therapist faces a most difficult problem. Super-reasonable people sit very still and upright; they move their faces very little, their voices are usually in a monotone, and they always talk very reasonably. You get this feeling of a kind of drying-up about the person; he or she is all locked in. As it happened, the father had been a Fundamentalist minister, and he had strong feelings about what was right and wrong. I noticed that he responded to all my overtures—the handshake, the questions, and the statements I made—in the same way. I felt that he listened, but I wasn't always sure he understood. I did find—and continue to find—that people who organize their responses in this fashion use lots of words to say things. It is important for me to try to tune in wherever I can in a way that is going to touch the person. And so when someone is organized by using big words and being reasonable, it is natural for me to come in on that level. Oftentimes therapists get bored by people who talk a lot. However, I need to have them talk enough so that I can understand what they are saying on the meta level. In the case of this man, he had told me about his repeated efforts to do what he wanted to do and how they continued to fail. Again, this was said in his dry, rather matter-of-fact voice. As I listened to him, I became aware that it sounded as though he had stopped trying. I asked him what had happened to his dreams. It sounded a little to me as if he had given up on his dreams. I began to see a light come into his eyes. The bottom half of his face didn't change particularly, but his eyes became a little wider and there was a little light in them. As I listened to his response, he said it was true that he didn't have any more dreams. They were dead.

In my mind, I now pictured him in a sculpture—a lifeless inner body with an outer hard shell. I use these stances and ways of communicating that I hear and see in my mind as my guidelines to the kinds of interventions I make with people. If this is done in a trusting, understanding, hearing context, then new understandings emerge. By the end of yesterday's interview, the husband's whole face was beginning to respond, not just his eyes.

I might say here—I think it is true of me and of others, too—that when I am listening to somebody, I am also looking at him or her and am aware of all his or her moving parts. I am aware of all the changes that may be going on. I am listening with my full self, with all of my senses.

There is an important element that I would like to mention. I call it the "energy field." I think it is important because it goes along with touching. Around any well-integrated person there is a circular field that is about three feet in diameter. At the edge of this field, you can feel vibrations—at least I can! These vibrations are like unacknowledged territorial lines around the person. When a person is relatively well put-together, those lines feel like elastic. If you come up to them, first of all you can physically feel them; you can feel that you are bumping against something. If it feels elastic, you know that you are there and that maybe you can reach over. I respect these lines. That's why I stay at arm's length. If I go closer to a person, I have already experimented as to whether or not his or her boundary will let me in. There seems to be a relation between the development of trust and the elasticity of this boundary.

When I am dealing with people who are very, very much out of contact with themselves, their energy field is only about two or three inches in diameter. I have to go a long way before I can feel any kind of vibration at all. It is a kind of deadness. I am virtually face to face with them before I get any kind of feeling of presence at all. When people have very violent insides, their field extends to about six feet and I am very aware of that. We tend to overuse the word *vibrations;* but I know what that feels like, and I am very respectful of that boundary. It is imaginary, but I can feel it in my body. When I'm around people in whom there is a lot of violence, I never go close until I can begin to feel the elasticity. I don't know if I am explaining this suitably, but it is a little like using your body to determine how far you can go. This is very relevant to the whole touching business because my touching doesn't take place unless I know that the other person's boundary is elastic.

Sight is also a part of this. The distance at which you can see someone—*really* see him—is probably nine or ten feet. At ten feet the outlines are there; the nuances are not there. You can see fairly well at six feet; at about three feet you can see much better. I want to get where I can be seen and heard as soon as I can. The process of going close is many times also the process of connecting—the slow way. You can't judge this by what you *should* do; you have to judge it by the way you feel. Some people who watched me work with a family and saw me touch said, "Aha! I see! All you have to do is touch." My answer was that touch has to be used just as carefully with people as with a hot stove. You are quite literally feeling your way. This is one of the reasons that when I work with therapists and train them, I try to train their body awareness. For example, when people get into murderous rages, it helps me to be in a position of helping but yet not crowding. I don't think the touch connection works in that kind of situation. Perhaps some of you have noticed that when someone is in a rage and you touch him or her, you might get hit. The hit is not because the person wants to kill you (although he or she could) but because at that time the boundaries have been violated.

I wondered then about the other members of yesterday's families and their dreams. For a few moments we talked about dreams that had not come to life. The wife's dream was of being able to have a life with her husband different from the one she had. She said she had started her marriage by always trying to please her husband. That had been what she was taught to do. She was now tired of it. I asked her if she would be willing to make a little picture with me. She agreed. I asked her to get down on her knees and to look up at her husband, whom I asked to stand on a stool. Then I asked the wife if what she was doing felt like anything she had ever felt before. She said that it did but she didn't want it to be like that anymore. Then I asked her husband how he felt up there, and he said he didn't like her being down there and he didn't like being on top. Then I asked them to fix it so they would both be comfortable. Of course, they ended up being eye-to-eye, both on the same level. It was following this that some expressions of hope began to appear on their faces.

What I want to emphasize here is that if I hear a person handling his or her responses in a super-reasonable fashion, I tune in at the level of the intellect but in such a way as to give the person an experience of really being heard and seen. If I shift to a person who—like yesterday's wife—is placating, I try to get in touch with what she hoped for herself and lead her to talk about some of her yearnings and loneliness. The wife did this, but it wouldn't have appeared unless I had asked.

With blamers—like the second oldest child—I have to get in touch with the longing to be connected. This was my approach yesterday when, rather than dealing with all the hate feelings, we focused instead on her own feelings about herself and her wish to be connected with her mother. What I found myself doing in each case was trying to help the person stabilize. Sometimes I did this with a touch of my hand, or perhaps just by getting the person to be physically still for a moment in order to focus.

This is important to share with you because as I sit with a family, my body tells me a great deal about where those people are and where their boundaries are. For example, the boundary is very, very close around a super-reasonable person. This is probably one of the reasons people say that the super-reasonable person is not "available." The boundary around an irrelevant person is all broken; you can't tell where it is. The boundary around a blamer is very far out and jagged. The placater is a very interesting person. His boundary is made out of liquid—out of whipped cream that is beginning to melt. It is there, but you can't tell much from it. Even though this is a somewhat picturesque way of talking about a person and his presence, it is something of which I am very aware, and I honor it. Perhaps a poetic way of putting it is this: What you are feeling at any point in time is how much of a person's life is willing to make itself known, with what fear, with what protectiveness. If you want to connect with that, you must be able to respect it.

My hands are my most valuable treatment asset. Also my body and my skin, in sensing what is going on; and my eyes in seeing; and the connections that all of these make. Hands are *so* important! This is one of the reasons I try to help people to educate their hands. Something else I do in affectional relationships with people is to help them to educate their bodies and also to be aware of space and boundaries. I am quite convinced that that's what this business of making connections really means. What I have just said helps me make a definition of *intimacy*. It is simply the freedom to respect the spaces between people—to go in when there is an invitation, and not to invade when there isn't one. That is real intimacy.

People often ask me, "How long is an interview?" It is as long as is necessary to make it possible to find and open a new window for people to look through. An interview can last anywhere from two to three hours. I am not doing office practice any more; when I was, I had three hours as my minimum time for an initial interview. I wanted people to leave the interview with something new that they could experiment with and live with. This means they go out of my office with a new awareness that they can use. It can be small or big, but that awareness carries with it some kind of hope—the hope that they can do something different about themselves, that life can be different for them in some way.

I timed the ensuing sessions to occur whenever another step was readying itself. This pattern is not rigid. My thought is that every interview has a life of its own. Nothing says that I am going to be around tomorrow to see you again or that you are going to be around. I work toward a new possibility and we have a closing on something as the family and I leave each other. That does not mean that all the work is finished. It never means that, because we can go on growing forever. But it does mean that at the end of the interview we have something new that can be useful.

For example, with the family I saw yesterday, the ending for me was my telling them that I enjoyed being with them and being a part of their life for two hours; and that I would have really liked to have been able to continue to be a part, but my life needs didn't make that possible. If by chance we were to meet again, I would like it very much. The idea is that an interview has a life of its own and the next interview will have still another life. Because if you are really growing, each interview will have still another life. Because if you are really growing, each interview is totally different. People are in different places and the therapist is in a different place. At any rate, that is how I like to look at it.

The promise I make to people is that I will tell them everything I can and show them everything I can. I cannot promise that I will tell *all* that is in me because I do not know that. I can tell you only what I know is there. Many of you who are reading may hear things that I never intended but that may be there anyway. My hope for you is that maybe you have found some new windows. Just as I did with the family yesterday, I have tried here to open some doors for you. I hope it will be useful.

PART FIVE: INVOLVING THE LARGER SYSTEM

An exciting challenge this past year (1981) allowed me to facilitate change more comprehensively than I have written about to this point. It was a chance to go beyond traditional conjoint family therapy and to involve the larger community.

Through the Family Institute of Virginia (under the direction of Joan Winter, M.S.W.), the Department of Corrections in the Commonwealth of Virginia undertook an extensive project to study the effectiveness of family therapy in treating juvenile delinquency. They chose three outstanding family therapists[1] who represented different schools of family therapy. Each of us was to design a program of treatment, enlist therapists we had trained, and supervise the implementation of our respective programs. There were sixty families in each of these three programs, and there also was a control group.

Some of the questions this study hoped to get data on were:

1. Could family therapy be effective in treating juvenile delinquency? If so, how?

---

[1]The other two therapists were Dr. Murray Bowen (of the Georgetown University Family Psychiatry Center) and Jay Haley (of the Family Therapy Institute in Washington, D.C.).

2. Did the therapists we selected differ from each other categorically? In other words, did the students who gravitated toward different schools of therapy have different psychological profiles?
3. What could each of the three orientations contribute to the treatment of the juvenile offender and his or her family?
4. Do therapists actually accomplish what they set out to do? (Since all our sessions were videotaped, we could compare the various interventions with their intent.)

A project of this kind has some potentially competitive aspects, and I felt it was important to avoid this so we could focus on contributions instead. I recognized the sincere desire of the juvenile justice department to find out how they could provide more meaningful service to their clients. It also seemed like an extraordinary opportunity for me to see new vistas. I would be able to see my work in a larger perspective.

None of the leaders would be doing therapy themselves. Our job was to design the treatment program and supervise our therapists. I designed my program to incorporate regular weekly contact with the probation officers, judges, and other community resources because I believed that all the points I could contact in the community system would be beneficial. It didn't seem to make much sense to see families without being in touch with this larger context and all the variables that have some impact on these families.

For the individual and family therapy sessions, I chose six therapists[2] who had studied with me: three men and three women who were competent as family therapists and experienced in living—"textured" by life, so to speak. I saw them as also being able to make a quick and strong connection with young people. These six did a superlative job.

In addition to the six therapists, I had three other people as part of the team. One was a pediatrician well versed in family therapy.[3] I wanted a physician to participate as a

---

[2]All six therapists, as well as the other members of my team, were members of the Avanta Network, a training program I created five years ago. The six therapists were: Ken Block, A.C.S.W., of Santa Cruz, California; Catherine Bond, M.A., of the Center for Counseling and Psychotherapy, in Santa Monica, California; Jack Dennis of San Diego, California; William Nerin, M.A., of Oklahoma City, Oklahoma; Anne Robertson, Ph.D., of Tiburon, California; and Marguerita Suarez, R.N., M.A., of the Northwest Center for Personal and Family Counseling, Inc., in Belleview, Washington.
[3]Jonathan Stoltzenberg, M.D., whose private practice in Hartford, Connecticut, is in developmental and behavioral pediatrics and medicine, and who is also on the faculty of the University of Connecticut Medical School.

cotherapist and consultant, especially in case family members responded with psychosomatic symptoms as the family system changed. I also wanted to ascertain whether there was a link between delinquent behavior and health, and whether the health of the family members improved as communication within the family improved. I believe that the body often says what the mouth cannot say.

The eighth team member[4] had a special interest in organizational development and worked with me as I contacted the juvenile justice system and other institutions. This person also acted as a liaison between my part of the project and the director of the project.

The ninth team member[5] had charge of the logistics of providing the support systems for the people in the project. The most demanding part of this job was coordinating the videotaping. Everything we did was videotaped, and families were encouraged to see the tapes of their sessions. The videotape "Family in Crisis," which shows how I work with a family, was also available to them. This was another of my ways to help people get information and gain confidence in undergoing treatment.

Because of my own time constraints and the fact that my office is in Menlo Park, California, I designed my program so that my team would come together in Richmond, Virginia, for a four-week period and treat all sixty families intensively, then break for four weeks and come back for a ten-day follow-up. I feel, in general, that intensive work over a short period of time is more effective than regular interviews over a protracted period, which is the traditional pattern.

As I had no facilities of my own in Virginia, all the family sessions took place in a large rented house. The ten of us on my team also lived there. This arrangement facilitated consultation and cotherapy. Living in such close proximity made it easy for the staff to maintain ongoing relationships with each other. It also provided a homey atmosphere for the families: they had room to relax. Tea, coffee, milk, and other refreshments were always available. I believe that a homey, welcoming, and relaxed context is a valuable adjunct to therapy.

It is my conviction that a group that works together needs to meet frequently for their personal and professional

---

[4]Jean Pickering, M.S.W., of Chapel Hill, North Carolina.
[5]Vernon Sparks, M.A., of Annapolis, Maryland.

growth. If the group members are open and available to each other, this is reflected in a markedly higher quality of therapy. This would hold true for staffs of mental health clinics, social agencies, and other community service groups.

I feel good about the selection of the six therapists, about how we lived and worked together, and about the emphasis on our support group. Good, solid family therapy was done. The family fact chronology and family maps were useful in treatment and in case supervision. Family sculpting was used a lot. However, each therapist had his or her own style. Flexibility —doing what was needed at the time—stands out in my mind as probably the most important factor. If we needed to provide transportation, we did; if we needed to see people in their homes, we did that, too. We did whatever had to be done to get families in and to help them grow.

Since I felt that a group learning experience for families would enrich the individual therapy sessions, I saw families in a large workshop on the weekends. These weekends were open to all concerned with the project: the treatment families, probation officers, judges, and other interested persons. I also did a total-community workshop for one day.

I am frequently asked how I conducted these large weekend meetings, which were attended by two to three hundred people and lasted four to six hours. As with many things I begin, I started out with the assumption that people were coming because they wanted something. Perhaps they were curious, wanted information, or needed help. Whatever it was, I was willing to help them get what they wanted. I had a hopeful attitude from the beginning. Regardless of whether they were aware of hope in themselves, I saw hope in them. I could be open with them, loving with them, and straight with them. My attitude of hope goes a long way toward helping people change. I am convinced that all people can grow. It is a matter of connecting them with their inner resources. That is the therapeutic task.

I had an advantage in that, prior to the first meeting of this treatment family group, all these people had neither met me before or had heard of me. The families in treatment had been sent my book *Peoplemaking,* which is the best book on my ideas about families. If the families had read *Peoplemaking* or had heard about it, they knew they would not be blamed; my books blame no one—certainly not parents—and this gives people a better feeling about coming to group sessions. It is an attitude that also acknowledges that I am dealing with intelligent people, which I think most people are (they just don't always act intelligently).

The meetings were held in a large room in a local church. We had moveable chairs and plenty of space. My opening was a warm, verbal greeting in which I said how glad I was to see everyone and that I hoped we could do some things together and learn something about how families worked. The thrust of these weekends was to learn how to live better within a family.

When the ambiance permitted, I asked whether there was anything anybody wanted to say, anything anybody wanted to do, or anything anybody wanted to find out. Then I waited: usually there would be no response for the first sixty seconds. I would encourage participation by noting, "You know, I bet no one ever asked you that question before. What do you want? What do you want for yourself?" (It's usually "What do you want for somebody else?")

Some brave soul would say, "I'd like to do something with my son" (or wife, husband, mother, or someone else). I accepted whatever was asked and reframed it to make it into a learning situation for the whole group.

I invited the questioner to come to the front of the room and be with me. Being within handshake distance of each other enabled that person and myself to experience each other's presence. I then developed an interaction, the meta message of which was one of acceptance of that person. For example, a man came up and said, "Well, my wife and I don't get along very well." I made the self-worth message explicit by saying, "First of all, I'd like you to give yourself a pat on the back for *saying* what you said." Articulating your feelings is the first step toward nurturing your self-esteem.

Then, to connect with the audience, I asked, "I'm curious as to whether anybody else in this group ever had any such trouble—you men, with your wives? [or vice versa]" Many hands went up. I find that the roots of all human problems are universal. There seem to be no exceptions, regardless of people's race, nationality, or economic status.

To turn this into a learning opportunity and also to proceed therapeutically, I said to this man, "Well, you're not alone, so maybe if you do something, the people out there will learn something, too." I have found that even when group members do not work specifically on themselves, they undergo many changes.

Then I proceeded to the specifics. "Now, tell me your name." He was named Carl. I shook his hand, being aware of what the handshake felt like. When and where you touch a stranger involves a delicate awareness of timing and a sense of that person's willingness to take risks. Touch is not a technique; it is a human connection (see the previous chapter, "When I Meet a Person").

In answer to the question "How are you feeling right *now?*" most volunteers would tell me they felt nervous. I would ask, "Where are you feeling nervous?" The answer might be that their knees were shaking. So I would say, "Well, let's shake them really good. I wonder if anybody else knows what it's like to feel nervous?" Of course, everybody did. "I know, too, so let's shake our knees." We'd both shake our knees; I would do so vigorously, as an example of making the forbidden and fearful grossly manifest (with a sense of humor). This allowed us to bring up the anxiety, shake it out, and be done with it.

"How are you feeling now?"

"Better."

"Good. Now, what was this that you said you wanted to do?"

"Well, my wife . . ."

"Why don't you ask her to come up and join you?" I asked. By that time, the wife was all ready to join. When she came up, I told the husband, "Before I go on with you, I want to meet your wife."

I turned toward her, smiled, and asked her name. "Hello, Sally. How did you feel when your husband came up here and did all the things that he did?" I did not ask her how she felt about his coming up to talk about "a problem," but instead asked how she felt about what he was doing here with me. Often the reply would be something like, "I never saw that in him before."

"That's kind of interesting," I said. "Maybe there are other parts you haven't noticed. I often find that's true." Then I spoke to Carl: "Do you think there could be parts to your wife that you haven't noticed yet?" He agreed there might be.

At this point, I was setting the stage for awakening inner resources. By this time, a tone of discovery (rather than blame) had been set. So I asked, "Well, Carl, what was it that you wanted to work on?"

"It has to do with her working late at night."

"What does that mean?" I asked.

"Well, she's home at eleven, and I get home at six. Then she sleeps in until seven, and I have to get up at four."

I said, "You're telling me you don't have much time together, and maybe you're also talking about time in bed. Is that what you're telling me?"

"Well, that's a piece of it."

I continued to explore until I found a basic but unspoken question: did his wife really care for him? If she really cared for him, she would change her hours. (The question almost always comes down to a self-esteem level: "Doing what I want you to do means you love me.")

His wife's answer was similar: "If he cared for me, he wouldn't prod me so much. Besides, sometimes he drinks too much."

Periodically, I would stop to ask the group, "Is this anything you know anything about?" Of course, 99 percent knew something about everything that Sally and Carl were talking about.

At this point, I chose to sculpt the communication. I introduced it by saying, "I've got an idea about something. Do you want to try it out with me?" With the couple's consent, I would say, "I've noticed something in your communication that I'd like to show you. I will make that picture with your bodies. Let me have your bodies for a while and I'll give them back to you"—I put a *lot* of humor in everything I do. Placing each of them in a physical blaming position, I asked, "Does that fit anything that goes on?"

"Oh, yes."

While they were in these positions, I asked each of them, "How does your body feel now?" As most people do, they reported body tensions, strains, fear, a decrease in breathing, etc. (I believe that the body is a metaphor for emotional expression.)

Then I asked, "What happens to break this up?"

"Well," Carl said, "the kids can break it up. Or I start to feel guilty."

"Are your kids here?"

"Yes."

"Well, let's ask them if they'd like to join us." The children agreed. After meeting and connecting with each of them, I continued with my family sculpting. I then asked each child, "Did you ever see your mother and father like this?"

"Yeah."

"What do each of you do when it's like that?"

One child went to stand by his mother. Another went to his father's side. Another said, "I just run out to the neighbor's." Everyone now had a graphic picture of this part of this family's interaction. It was equally clear how this kind of communication could get them into trouble.

We continued the sculpting, changing positions and talking about how each person felt. I was working with the family, with the family process, and, on another level, with the whole group.

Humor is a very important part of my work. I come into the group with a real feeling—a *bone* feeling—that I am going to meet people and that people, for me, are capable of all kinds of transformations. I believe that everyone is teachable. I constantly model how things that are heavy can be talked about in a light way. If I feel that a story, an analogy, or a caricature would be useful, I stop and share it. Often, stories can carry a point much more effectively than straight dialogue.

Interspersed with personal work in these large groups, I did some exercises. I broke up the group into pairs, triads, or small groups. One result of these exercises is that people make contact with other people and feel supported; at the same time, they learn new ways of experiencing themselves and others. I have many exercises, and I feel free to design whatever I think will fit.[6]

At some point, I lead the members of each workshop in a centering exercise, which I label in various ways: relaxation, stress reduction, or meditation. I ask people to get in a comfortable physical position, close their eyes, and be in touch with their breathing, and I lead them into a journey designed to give them good feelings about themselves. I believe that people can handle tough problems more creatively when they feel good about themselves. (I have found it helpful to do this exercise in individual family sessions as well.) It is a good way to begin and end the group session.

The work done in the large weekend groups in Virginia augmented the work in the individual family sessions. Attendance was encouraged and was voluntary; about 35 percent of the families in treatment attended regularly. I am writing about the large groups in some detail because I have not described them elsewhere, and I thought they might be new to many of you. The large group meeting takes the burden off the patient and his or her family because the problems become universal: the areas of self-worth, communication, and appreciation of differences concern the entire group. I hope others will experiment with this modality.

The final results from the project in Richmond, Virginia,

---

[6]See the Author's Note at the end of this book regarding my communication videotapes, which contain many exercises.

are not yet in. There will be a two-year follow-up and, in the end, we may learn much more than I have written about here. Nevertheless, I could see that my group had an enormous impact on the families, the juvenile judicial system, and to some extent on the community, which gave us great response: the local newspapers and radio stations gave us good publicity, and many people from the general public attended the community workshop.

I feel good about our decision to work intensively for a short period of time. I think we started some changes that will evolve on their own. I would have like to continue longer. However, from a research point of view, we might learn more about this intensive, short-term approach that could help us affirm the inherent strength in families, especially when the larger system has been modified.

I am also glad the study was so thorough and had such a well-thought-out research design. I think the results will show we had an enormous impact at the individual, family, institutional, and community levels. If my impressions are confirmed, perhaps there will be replications in other states and extensions of this approach.

AUTHOR'S NOTE

Some of you may want to know more about my theory and practice. People who have read this book often ask, "What do I do next?"

I have been teaching family therapy much of my professional life, but I have not written books or produced materials with an overall format in mind that goes from elementary to advanced theory and practice. During the years I was teaching, I was also learning and modifying my ideas. In fact, some of the most important processes that I use in training and in doing therapy, such as Family Reconstruction and Parts Parties, have not yet been written about in a way that is available to the general reader. I hope to pull together this more advanced material in the near future. Meanwhile, here is my advice about what to do with what is currently available.

I recommend that you read my book *Peoplemaking* (if you have not already done so) both for personal growth and to learn the communication stances that are mentioned only briefly in this book. Experiencing personal growth while learning specific techniques continues throughout all the teaching I do. Both are essential. Whenever possible, I try to provide an opportunity for the student to experience what I am trying to teach. As an example in this regard, you will find a number of communication exercises in *Peoplemaking*. Please do them with your family if possible.

The following recommendations are not in specific order. You might want to read *Changing with Families,* which I coauthored with Richard Bandler and John Grinder. I now think of that book as an elaboration of some of the ideas I have presented in *Conjoint Family Therapy* (particularly in chapters IX and X).

In the book *Helping Families to Change,* which I coauthored with James Stachowiak and Harvey Taschman, you will find a chapter on simulated families that is particularly useful if you are doing any teaching.

Family in Crisis* is a videotape that follows the treatment of a family over a period of eight months. The emphasis is on my first session with the family, in which the Identified Patient has an epileptic seizure that clearly seems triggered by the changes I am bringing about in the family system. The tape also shows one form of cotherapy: Dr. Dewitt (Bud) Baldwin and I worked together.

My videotapes *Communication I** and *Communication II** were produced from workshops I gave at the University of Manitoba. They cover many of the ideas that will be familiar to those who have read *Conjoint Family Therapy* and *Peoplemaking,* such as an individual's "pot," his or her awareness and acceptance of feelings and their relationship to communication, congruence, double-level messages, "Hanging Hats," peripheral space, "making meaning," and so forth. Moreover, the tapes show a number of very useful experiences. I divide a large college audience into small groups for a personal experience of some of these concepts, and the methods I use can be adapted to many teaching situations. They may also stimulate you to think of how to translate theory into practice for families you are treating.

I have written three shorter books: *Making Contact, Self-Esteem,* and *Your Many Faces.* These are relatively inexpensive, and families may find them useful.

Michele Baldwin and I are currently collaborating with Bud Baldwin on a book tentatively titled *Satir Step by Step.* It follows the transcript of a therapy session and, as the title implies, makes explicit what I am doing. Students and therapists alike should find it instructive and helpful.

---

*Available from Science and Behavior Books, Inc.

At some point, perhaps after reading *Peoplemaking,* you may decide to undertake fairly intensive training in my method. I recommend that you write to the Avanta office at P.O. Box 7402, Menlo Park, CA 94025, to find out about training opportunities with members of the Avanta Network (formerly the Humana Network). This is a project I founded in 1976 because of the many requests I had received for a training program. Avanta members are highly trained, competent teachers of family systems; some of them may be available in your community.

If possible, try to attend a Process Community. This is an Avanta program of three to four weeks. Its intensive training combines personal growth with the study of specific techniques and utilizes Parts Parties, Family Reconstruction, and experience in working in triads and with large groups.

As you can see, I do not recommend a specific time table for all of this. Take what fits as you sense the need.

BIBLIOGRAPHY

I regard books as inspirations to new possibilities, springboards to trying out new things, and resources to add to information. By the nature of things, books represent the part of the world that the writer sees and how that world is interpreted. I enjoy seeing the various ways people view the same things.

In addition to the references cited in this book, this selected reading list includes books and articles that have been particularly exciting, inspiring, and informational for me. I have grouped them so that you, the reader, might more quickly locate your special interests.

Children

1. Bartz, Wayne R., and Richard A. Rasor. *Surviving With Kids.* San Luis Obispo, CA: Impact Publishers, 1978.
2. Black, Claudia. *My Dad Loves Me, My Dad has a Disease.* Newport Beach, CA: Alcoholism, Children & Therapy, 1979.
3. Nicholson, Luree, and Laura Torbet. *How to Fight Fair with Your Kids and Win.* New York: Harcourt, Brace, Jovanovich, 1980.
4. Pearce, Joseph Childton. *The Magical Child: Rediscovering Nature's Plan for Our Children.* New York: E. P. Dutton, 1977.
5. Percy, Bernard, ed. *How to Grow a Child.* Los Angeles, CA: Price/Stein/Sloan, 1978.
6. Rose, Anthony L., and Andre Auw. *Growing Up Human.* New York: Harper & Row, 1974.

Couple Relationships

7. Brandon, Nathaniel. *The Psychology of Romantic Love.* Los Angeles, CA: J. P. Tarcher, 1980.
8. Garland, Diana R. *Couples Communication and Negotiation Skills.* Workshop Models for Family Life Education Series. New York: Family Service Assn. of America, 1978.
9. Kilgore, James E. *Try Marriage before Divorce.* Waco, TX: Word Books, 1978.
10. Koch, Joanne, and Lou Koch. *The Marriage Savers.* New York: Coward, McCann & Geoghegan, 1976.
11. Lederer, William J., and Don D. Jackson. *Mirages of Marriage.* New York: Norton, 1968.
12. Miller, Sherod; Elam W. Nunnally; and Danile B. Wackman. *Alive and Aware.* Minneapolis, MN: Interpersonal Communication Programs, 1975.
13. Pelton, Charles L. *The Sex Book for Those Who Think They Know It All.* Aberdeen, SD: C. L. Pelton, 1980.
14. Shostrom, Everett, and James Kavanaugh. *Between Man and Woman: The Dynamics of Interpersonal Relationships.* Los Angeles, CA: Nash Publishing, 1971.

15. Smith, Gerald Walker. *Hidden Meanings.* New York: Peter H. Wyden, 1975.

Divorce

16. Coogler, O. J. *Structure Mediation in Divorce Settlements: A Handbook for Marital Mediators.* Lexington, MA: Lexington Books, 1978.
17. Gettleman, Susan, and Janet Markowitz. *The Courage to Divorce.* New York: Simon & Schuster, 1974.
18. Haynes, John M. *Divorce Mediation: A Practical Guide for Therapists and Counselors.* New York: Springer Publishing, 1981.
19. Smoke, Jim. *Growing through Divorce.* Irvine, CA: Harvest House, 1976.

Family Process and Family Therapy

20. Ackerman, Nathan. *Psychodynamics of Family Life.* New York: Basic Books, 1958.
21. ———. "Behavior Trends and Disturbances of the Contemporary Family" in I. Galdston, ed., *The Family in Contemporary Society.* New York: International Universities Press, 1958.
22. Bateson, G. "A Theory of Play and Fantasy." *Psychiat. Res. Rep.* 2 (1955):39–51.
23. ———; D. D. Jackson; J. Haley; and J. H. Weakland. "Toward a Theory of Schizophrenia." *Behav. Sci.* 1 (1956):251–64.
24. Borzormengi, Nagy, ed., and James L. Tramo. *Intensive Family Therapy.* New York: Harper & Row, 1965.
25. Bowen, Murray A. "A Family Concept of Schizophrenia," in D. Jackson, ed., *The Etiology of Schizophrenia.* New York: Basic Books, 1960.
26. ———. *Family Therapy in Clinical Practice.* New York: Aronson, Jason, 1978.
27. Brodey, Warren M. "Some Family Operations of Schizophrenia: A Study of Five Hospitalized Families Each with a Schizophrenic Member." *Arch. Gen. Psychiat.* 1 (1959):379–402.
28. Cantor, David, and William Lehr. *Inside the Family.* San Francisco, CA: Jossey-Bass, 1975.
29. Corales, Ramon, and Charles B. Bernard. *Theory and Techniques of Family Therapy.* Springfield, IL: Charles C. Thomas, 1979.

30. Dodson, Laura Sue. *Family Counseling: A Systems Approach.* DeWayne Kurpius, ed. Muncie, IN: Accelerated Development, 1977.

31. Grindler, John; Richard Bandler; and Virginia Satir. *Changing with Families.* Palo Alto, CA: Science & Behavior Books, 1976.

32. Haley, Jay. "Control in the Psychotherapy of Schizophrenics." *Arch. Gen. Psychiat.* 5 (1961):340–53.

33. ———. "The Family of the Schizophrenic: A Model System." *J. Nerv. Ment. Dis.* 129 (1959):357–74.

34. ———. "An Interactional Description of Schizophrenia." Psychiatry 22 (1959):321–32.

35. ———. *Uncommon Therapy: The Psychiatric Techniques of Milton H. Erickson, M.D.* New York: Norton, 1977.

36. Jackson, Don D. "Action for Mental Illness—What Kind?" *Stanford Medical Bulletin* 20 (1962):77–80.

37. ———. "Family Interaction, Family Homeostasis, and Some Implications for Conjoint Family Psychotherapy" in J. Masserman, ed., *Individual and Familial Dynamics.* New York: Grune & Stratton, 1959.

38. ———. "A Note on the Genesis of Trauma in Schizophrenia." *Psychiatry* 20 (1957):181–84.

39. ———. "The Question of Family Homeostasis." *Psychiat. Quart. Suppl.* 31 (1957):79–90; first presented at APA, St. Louis, 1954.

40. ———; J. Riskin; and Virginia Satir. "A Method of Analysis of a Family Interview." *Arch. Gen. Psychiat.* 5 (1961):321–39.

41. ———, and Virginia Satir. "Family Diagnosis and Family Therapy," in N. Ackerman et al., *Exploring the Base for Family Therapy.* New York: Family Service Assn., 1961.

42. ———, and J. H. Weakland. "Conjoint Family Therapy: Some Considerations on Theory, Technique, and Results." *Psychiatry* 24 (1961), suppl. to No. 2:30–45.

43. Lewis, O. *The Children of Sanchez: Autobiography of a Mexican Family.* New York: Random House, 1961.

44. Lidz, Theodore; A. Cornelison; S. Fleck; and D. Terry. "The Intrafamilial Environment of Schizophrenic Patients: II. Marital Schism and

Marital Skew." *Amer. J. Psychiat.* 114
(1959):241–48.

45. ———. "The Intrafamilial Environment of Schizophrenic
Patients: VI. Transmission of Irrationality." *Arch.
Neurol. Psychiat.* 79 (1958):305–16.

46. Luthman, Shirley, and Martin Kirschenbaum. *The
Dynamic Family.* Palo Alto, CA: Science &
Behavior Books, 1974.

47. MacGregor, Robert; Agnes M. Ritchie; Alberto C. Serrano;
and Franklin P. Schuster, Jr. *Multiple-Impact
Therapy with Families.* New York: McGraw Hill,
1964.

48. Minuchin, Salvador. *Families and Family Therapy.*
Cambridge, MA: Harvard University Press, 1974.

49. ——— et al. *Families of the Slums: An Exploration of
their Structure Treatment.* New York: Basic
Books, 1967.

50. ———, and H. Charles Fishman. *Family Therapy
Techniques.* Cambridge, MA: Harvard University
Press, 1981.

51. ———. *Psychosomatic Families: Anorexia Nervosa in
Context.* Cambridge, MA: Harvard University
Press, 1978.

52. Pemberton, W. H. "Nondirective Reorientation in
Counseling." *ETC* 16 (1959):407–16.

53. Perls, Frederick S. *Gestalt Therapy Verbatim.* Moab, UT:
Real People Press, 1969.

54. Perls, Fritz. *The Gestalt Approach and Eye Witness to
Therapy.* New York: Bantam Books, 1976.

55. Satir, Virginia; James Stachowiak; and Harvey A.
Taschman. *Helping Families to Change.* New
York: Jacob Aronson, 1977.

56. Scheflen, Albert E. *Levels of Schizophrenia.* New York:
Brunner-Mazel, 1981.

57. Wegscheider, Sharon. *Another Chance: Hope and Health
for Alcoholic Families.* Palo Alto, CA: Science &
Behavior Books, 1981.

58. Wittaker, Carl, and Augustus Y. Napier. *The Family
Crucible: An Intensive Experience in Family
Therapy.* New York: Harper & Row, 1978.

Holistic Health

59. Brown, Barbara. *Supermind: The Ultimate Energy.* New
York: Harper & Row, 1980.

60. Cousins, Norman. *The Anatomy of an Illness*. New York: W. W. Norton, 1979.
61. ———. *The Celebration of Life: Dialogue on Immortality and Infinity*. New York: Harper & Row, 1974.
62. Green, Elmer, and Alyce Green. *Beyond Biofeedback*. New York: Delacorte, 1977.
63. Ostrander, Sheila; Lynn Schroeder; with Nancy Ostrander. *Superlearning*. New York: Delacorte/Confucian, 1979.
64. Pelletier, Kenneth R. *Holistic Medicine*. New York: Delacorte, 1980.
65. ———. *Mind as Healer, Mind as Slayer: A Holistic Approach to Preventing Stress Disorders*. New York: Delacorte/Delta, 1977.
66. Shealy, Norman. *Ninety Days to Self Health: Biogenics*. New York: Dial, 1977.
67. Simonton, Carl, and Stephanie Simonton. *Getting Well Again*. New York: Bantam, 1980.

General Issues re: The Family

68. Bateson, G. "Language and Psychotherapy: Frieda Fromm-Reichmann's Last Project." *Psychiatry* 21 (1958):96–100.
69. Bell, N. W., and E. F. Vogel, eds. *The Family*. Glencoe, IL: Free Press, 1960.
70. Berne, E. *Transactional Analysis*. New York: Grove Press, 1961.
71. Benson, Jeanette, and Jack L. Hilyard. *Becoming Family*. Winoana, MN: St. Mary's College Press, 1978.
72. Boston Women's Health Collective. *Ourselves, Our Children*. New York: Random House, 1978.
73. Davis, Bruce, and Jenny Wright. *Hugs and Kisses*. New York: Workman, 1977.
74. Fromm, E. *The Art of Loving*. New York: Harper & Row, 1956.
75. Kilgore, James, with Don Highlander. *Getting More Family out of Your Dollar*. Irvine, CA: Harvest House, 1974.
76. LeBoyer, Frederick. *Inner Beauty, Inner Light*. New York: Knopf, 1978.
77. Montague, Ashley. *Touching: The Human Significance of the Skin*. New York: Columbia University Press, 1971.

78. Schwab, Johanna. *Family Communication Program.*
     Menlo Park, CA: California National Family
     Communication Center, 1972.
79. Stinnett, Nick, and James Walter. *Relationships in
     Marriage and Family.* New York: Macmillan,
     1977.
80. Wegscheider, Don. *If Only My Family Understood Me . . .*
     Minneapolis, MN: CompCare Publications, 1979.

Blended Families

81. Lewis, Helen C. *All About Families: The Second Time.*
     Atlanta, GA: Peachtree Publishers, 1980.
82. Kilgore, James. *Try Marriage before Divorce.* Waco, TX:
     Word Books, 1978.
83. Kirk, II. David. *Shared Fate.* New York: Free Press, 1964.
84. Ricci, Isolina. *Mom's House, Dad's House: Making Joint
     Custody Work.* New York: Macmillan, 1980.
85. Simon, Ann W. *Stepchild in the Family.* Indianapolis, IN:
     Odyssey Press/Bobbs-Merrill, 1964.
86. Thomson, Helen. *The Successful Stepparent.* New York:
     Harper & Row, 1966.
87. Visher, Emily B., and John S. Visher. *Stepfamilies.* New
     York: Brunner/Mazel Publishing, 1979.

One-Parent Families

88. Gately, Richard, and David Koulack. *The Single Father's
     Handbook.* New York: Anchor/Doubleday, 1979.

Personal Growth

89. Assagioli, Roberto. *Act of Will.* New York: Penguin, 1974.
90. Barbach, Lonnie Garfield. *For Yourself.* New York:
     Doubleday, 1975.
91. Bernhard, Yetta. *How to Be Somebody.* Millbrae, CA:
     Celestial Arts, 1975.
92. ———. *Self-Care.* Millbrae, CA: Celestial Arts, 1975.
93. Berzon, Betty, and Robert Leighton. *Positively Gay.*
     Millbrae, CA: Celestial Arts, 1979.
94. Bonny, Helen, and Lou Savory. *Music and Your Mind:
     Listening with a New Consciousness.* New York:
     Harper & Row, 1973.
95. Boren, James H. *When in Doubt, Mumble: A Bureaucrat's*

    Handbook. New York: Van Nostrand Reinhold, 1972.

96. Bresler, David, and Richard Trubo. *Free Yourself from Pain.* New York: Pocket Books, 1980.

97. Briggs, Dorothy Corkille. *Celebrate Yourself.* New York: Doubleday, 1977.

98. Buzan, Tony. *Use Both Sides of Your Brain.* New York: E. P. Dutton, 1974.

99. Camiel, Reva, and Hila Michaelsen. *First Time Out: Skills for Living Away from Home.* Sacramento, CA: Jalmar Press, 1980.

100. Clark, Don. *Loving Someone Gay.* Millbrae, CA: Celestial Arts, 1977.

101. Colton, Helen. *Adults Need Sex Education, Too.* Los Angeles, CA: Family Forum (1539 Courtney Avenue, CA 90046), n.d.

102. de Castillejo, Irene Claremont. *Knowing Woman: A Feminine Psychology.* New York: Harper & Row/Colophon, 1973.

103. Edwards, Betty. *Drawing on the Right Side of the Brain: A Course in Enhancing Creativity and Artistic Confidence.* Los Angeles: J. P. Tarcher, 1979.

104. Enelow, Gertrude. *The Joy of Physical Freedom.* Chicago, IL: Henry Regnery Co., 1973.

105. Gale, Raymond F. *Who Are You?* Englewood Cliffs, NJ: Prentice Hall, 1976.

106. Greenwald, Jerry. *Be the Person You Were Meant to Be: Antidotes to Toxic Living.* New York: Simon & Schuster, 1973.

107. Hayakawa, S. I. *Symbol, Status and Personality.* New York: Harcourt, Brace & World, 1963.

108. ———. *The Use and Misuse of Language.* Greenwich, CT: Fawcett Publications/Premier Books, 1962.

109. Huxley, A. *The Art of Seeing.* New York: Harper, 1942.

110. James, Muriel, and Dorothy Jongeward. *Born to Win.* Menlo Park, CA: Addison-Wesley, 1971.

111. Jampolsky, Gerald. *Love Is Letting Go of Fear.* New York: Bantam, 1981.

112. Johnson, Vernon E. *I'll Quit Tomorrow.* New York: Harper & Row, 1973.

113. Kubler-Ross, Elizabeth. *On Death and Dying.* New York: Macmillan, 1969.

114. Lair, Jess. *I Ain't Much Baby, But I'm All I Got.* Garden City, NY: Doubleday, 1972.

115. Lakien, Alan. *How to Get Control of Your Time and Your Life.* New York: NAL/Signet, 1974.
116. Larsen, Tony. *Trust Yourself.* San Luis Obispo, CA: Impact Publishers, 1979.
117. Leite, Evelyn. *To Be Somebody.* Center City, MN: Hazelden Foundation, 1979.
118. MacKensie, Alec. *The Time Trap.* New York: McGraw-Hill, 1975.
119. Masters, Robert, and Jean Houston. *Listening to the Body: The Psychological Way to Health and Awareness.* New York: Delta Books/Dell, 1978.
120. Mendino, O. G. *The Greatest Gift in the World.* New York: Frederick Fell, 1968.
121. Paulist, Trina. *Hope for the Flowers.* New York: Paulist Press, 1972.
122. Rainwater, Janette. *You're in Charge.* Los Angeles, CA: Guild of Tutors Press, 1979.
123. Rama, Swami; Rudolph Ballentine; and Alan Hymes. *Science of Breath: A Practical Guide.* Honesdale, PA: Himalayan Institute of Yoga Science & Philosophy, 1979.
124. Satir, Virginia. *Making Contact.* Millbrae, CA: Celestial Arts, 1976.
125. ———. *Peoplemaking.* Palo Alto, CA: Science & Behavior Books, 1972.
126. ———. *Self-Esteem.* Millbrae, CA: Celestial Arts, 1975.
127. ———. *Your Many Faces.* Millbrae, CA: Celestial Arts, 1978.
128. Scheele, Adele M. *Skills for Success: A Guide to the Top.* New York: William Morrow, 1979.
129. Schwartz, Jackie. *Letting Go of Stress.* New York: Pinnacle, 1982.
130. Schwarz, Jack. *Path of Action.* New York: Dutton, 1977.
131. Selye, Hans. *Stress without Distress.* Philadelphia, PA: J. B. Lippincott, 1974.
132. ———. *The Stress of Life.* Philadelphia, PA: J. B. Lippincott, 1956.
133. Shelly, Maynard, and Johanna Buck. *How to Be Happy, Happier, Happiest.* New York: Chatham Square Press, 1977.
134. Phelps, Stanlee, and Nancy Austin. *The Assertive Woman.* Fredericksburg, VA: Book Crafters, 1975.
135. Virshup, Evelyn. *Right Brain People in a Left Brain World.* Los Angeles, CA: Guild of Tutors Press, 1978.

136. Watts, A. W. *Nature, Man and Woman.* New York: Pantheon Books, 1958.
137. ———. *Psychotherapy East and West.* New York: Pantheon Books, 1961.
138. Watzlawick, P. *An Anthology of Human Communication.* Palo Alto, CA: Science & Behavior Books, 1963.
139. ———; J. Beavin; D. Jackson. *Pragmatics of Human Communication.* New York: W. W. Norton, 1967.
140. Wood, John T. *How Do You Feel?* Englewood Cliffs, NJ: Prentice-Hall, 1974.
141. ———. *What Are You Afraid Of?* Englewood Cliffs, NJ: Prentice-Hall, 1976.
142. Wysor, Bettie. *The Lesbian Myth: Insights and Conversation.* New York: Random House, 1974.

INDEX